FRONTIERS OF ACCESS TO LIBRARY MATERIALS
No. 2

FRONTIERS OF ACCESS TO LIBRARY MATERIALS

Sheila S. Intner, Series Editor

Collection Development and Finance: A Guide to Strategic Library-Materials Budgeting

Murray S. Martin

American Library Association
Chicago and London 1995

Cover designed by Richmond Jones

Composed by Publishing Services, Inc., Bettendorf, Iowa
   in Caslon on Xyvision/Linotype L330

Printed on 60-pound Authors B-05, a pH-neutral stock,
   and bound in 10-point C1S cover stock by
   Malloy Lithographing, Inc.

The paper used in this publication meets the minimum requirements of
American National Standard for Information Sciences—Permanence of
Paper for Printed Library Materials, ANSI Z39.48-1992.∞

Library of Congress Cataloging-in-Publication Data

Martin, Murray S.
    Collection development and finance : a guide to strategic library-
materials budgeting / by Murray S. Martin.
        p.   cm. — (Frontiers of access to library materials: no. 2)
    Includes bibliographical references and index.
    ISBN 0-8389-0648-6 (alk. paper)
    1. Library materials budgets—United States. 2. Collection develop-
ment (Libraries)—United States. I. Title. II. Series.
Z689.5.U6M37   1995
025.2′187073—dc20   94-49211

Printed in the United States of America

99 98 97 96 95   5 4 3 2 1

Contents

Tables

Figures

Preface

For many years I have been interested in library finance. As both a librarian and an accountant, I have been able to bring to library budgets a binocular view (to borrow a literary term), aware of the need to implement a program and the need to adhere to accounting rules. As a part-time literary scholar, I am also aware of the effects of both on the user.

It has become fashionable to look at libraries from a business point of view—too fashionable perhaps, when such a view fails to take into account the long-term goals which are at the heart of collection development. Business-oriented perspectives tend to focus upon year-end profits and balance sheets rather than long-term investments. To serve its user community, any library must amass resources, trusting that, in doing so, the right choices have been made. The match between today's fiscal demands and tomorrow's scholarly or information demands is never easy to achieve. Librarians must continually choose between equal goods and are only too aware of the fragility of the support on which they must depend.

Being aware of, and sensitive to the needs and often peremptory demands of other administrators, librarians become sensitive to the importance of each decision they make. As the needs of users grow and budgets shrink, librarians have the unenviable task of trying to seek a balance, one that will meet what they know to be long-term needs and what they often find are transitory financial pressures.

Library collections are forever. Although the fact is not often stressed, the writings of thousands of years past are still important, still relevant to today's needs. Modern society is fascinated by the great changes in technology, and many administrators mistakenly believe that all those wonderful electronic media will make the traditional library, with its inordinate financial demands, obsolete. Nothing could be further from the truth. Yes, there *are* new ways of packaging and transferring information, but using them requires the same skills of selection, acquisition, and organization that the older media do. No budget is ever large enough to meet the voracious demands of users. Libraries will continue to have to balance formats and modes of access to meet those needs. This process will require the same budgetary skills that it has in the past. There is, even among librarians, the feeling that "access" and "information" have made those traditional skills less meaningful, as if providing access did not demand even more of the skills of selectors and acquisition librarians, as well as calling into the picture even more librarians, such as those in lending services and interlibrary loan. Access as such is beyond the scope of this book, but reference will be made as appropriate to its effects on library materials budgets.

This book is dedicated to the many librarians who have, over the years, by acquisition or borrowing, tried to satisfy the needs of library users. That number includes not only those who have grappled with the problems of collection development and acquisition, but also those who toil to make resource sharing more than an empty phrase, those who conduct database searches, and those who must explain why something that is so urgently needed simply is not available. Instant gratification is perhaps a hallmark of modern American society and, by extension, all those societies which seek to emulate America. This book is also dedicated to those who have chosen librarianship as a career in perhaps the most difficult of times. I hope it will help them to see how an understanding of financial practice can make their work easier.

The basic lesson is that gratification may sometimes have to be delayed, but the library is in the business of ensuring that real needs can be met. This may be small comfort to librarians who are in the battle lines, but, taking a longer perspective, libraries are assured of a continuing place in the information world. With apologies to Voltaire, if libraries did not exist we should be compelled to invent them.

My special thanks to Sheila Intner, whose unflagging encouragement helped me through writer's block, and who provided excellent editorial direction. My thanks also to Mary Huchting and other staff members who helped turn the manuscript into a publishable book. Any errors remaining are certainly mine.

Chapter 1

Collections and Finance: Interrelationships

Too often a library's collections are thought of as something apart from the rest of the institution. True, they are seen as central to the library's mission, but it is almost as if they came into being spontaneously. They are, in fact, the product of years of work by many people and the result of the expenditure of large sums of money.

In a college or university setting, the library may well be the largest single financial investment. In a city or a township, the collections represent a sizable investment of public money. In both settings, the library and its collections continue well beyond the time of any single administration, and they represent the continuity of the community. To maintain such a library requires ongoing investment, in much the same way as buildings need to be repaired and renovated, or streets need to be repaved. The value of planned collections far exceeds their actual cost, and keeping them current enhances that value.

The interconnection between the investment of money and the value of collections is seldom studied. For an exception, see the concept of value maintenance in Dunn and Martin.[1] More emphasis is given in the literature to the policies and procedures designed to promote collection development and management. Yet, over the years, the availability or not of money, and the wisdom used in its expenditure, have shaped those collections. Among the guidelines published by the Association for Library Collections and Technical Services there are guidelines for the allocation of money.[2] Allocation, however, is not the only financial aspect of collection management. Financial considerations also include the monitoring of materials expenditures and their relationship to the general library budget.

Much has been written about the problems caused by rapidly rising serials costs.[3] For all this concern, however, there has been little interest in revisiting the budgetary assumptions that underlie most library budgets. Jerry Campbell has questioned the wisdom of the 60/40 split,[4] and there have been some discussions of the likely new role of electronic access.[5] Apart from these scattered publications, there is little that examines the close connection between financial management and collection development.

Policies for collection development, weeding, and the like, while essential as management tools, are simply statements of ideals and goals. They are given reality by the daily activities of many individuals. Those actions, in turn, are controlled by the availability of money. In times of financial retrenchment, the library budget may be as potent a driving force as any policy statement. It is not without significance that 40 percent of the college presidents polled in a 1992 *U.S. News and World Report* survey saw the reduction of library acquisitions as one way of controlling financial growth. Just as potentially troublesome is the fact that even more saw it necessary to control nonfaculty personnel expenditures and to reduce administrative costs.[6] No doubt some of this talk simply reflects current business fads, but together these ideas suggest that libraries must rethink their goals and options and at the same time prepare much stronger defenses of their necessity.

Financial Aspects of Resource Sharing

From another perspective, librarians and administrators alike have been assailed by the endless promotion of electronic alternatives. In library terms, this development becomes a battle between access and ownership. Too few have realized, first, that access implies ownership—by someone else—and, second, that access may not be the answer to basic everyday needs. This caution was well expressed by Jim Traue, former Turnbull Librarian in Wellington, New Zealand: he said this situation suggests Langdon Winner's "information myth," in which undefined access to undefined information empowers everyone—effortlessly.[7] Access has taken on the feel of an easy technological fix, one which will be costless and painless, unlike the continuing financial needs of a library. These comments underline the political nature of decision making and the ways various coalitions can influence what happens to the library.

What must a library do to balance these conflicting forces while still pursuing its basic goal of making information readily available in a timely fashion to those who need it? No library can possibly be self-sufficient; it must rely on its ability to cooperate with other libraries or agencies. While much lip service has been paid to resource sharing, few have investigated the mechanisms and the costs involved. Other than the interminable studies of interlibrary loan, little attention has been directed to shared collection development[8] and even less to the actual costs of electronic networks, document retrieval, or contracted services. Almost nothing has been done to modify the old formulas (*pace* Clapp-Jordan[9]), which were almost exclusively concerned with the purchase and ownership of printed books and serials.

Any policy on collection development or resource allocation which overlooks or neglects the costs of access and resource sharing will provide a library only with a guide to insignificance. There is still, for every library, a basic need to provide frequently used materials on site. There is also the need to provide rules and finance for access to the wider range of materials that cannot be locally owned. There will still be libraries dedicated to developing comprehensive collections in closely defined areas, and the major research libraries of the country will continue to collect against tomorrow's needs, but most other libraries have to make agonizing choices between equally valued acquisitions.

Finance, for these reasons, plays as large a role in the library world as the formulation of policies.[10] The basic question is how best to use the available funds. Answering it may require rethinking all basic premises. It may also require a much more stringent examination of priorities and alternatives than is customarily executed.

Budgetary Concepts

A long-standing problem has been the virtual separation of the library materials budget from other parts of the library budget. This custom has always been shortsighted, since the acquisition of a certain flow or mix of materials has always carried with it other costs—acquisition, processing, and shelving, to name only the most obvious. When we must also consider the effects of access or information on demand, these relationships become even more central to library budgeting.

Not only must libraries look at the absolute costs of obtaining materials by acquisition, interlibrary loan, or electronic transfer; they must also look at the comparative costs, and their relationship to the library's goals and priorities.[11] These costs have short- and long-term implications. In the short term, it may pay to borrow materials at a transaction cost which, while still high, is lower than the cost of purchasing. In the long term, such a policy, pushed to extremes, will weaken substantially the collections which must remain the core of user services. Moreover, the success of the strategy depends on being sure that other libraries or agencies have made decisions in favor of ownership. There are two issues here. First is the need to ensure that the whole range of information will be available somewhere. Second is the need to take care that decisions about the relative importance of various materials are not taken out of the hands of the library. It is only too easy for a supplier of information to restrict the amount of information available to that which is financially profitable, leaving libraries to scramble in the dark for the more arcane needs of their users.

If the library world is not to be divided even more sharply into haves and have-nots, all libraries must be prepared to look seriously at the relationships between finance and policy.

Accountability

A final consideration is one that affects librarians directly. The modern push for accountability requires that all librarians must be able to show that they are spending their budgets wisely. Since library materials (owned or accessed) will still account for a major proportion of all library budgets, librarians must be able to show that their policies, choices, and procedures have been properly conceived and adequately monitored.

Accountability implies not only setting up a budget that reflects goals and priorities, but also monitoring it to see that those goals and objectives are being met. The road to the latter goal is not always smooth. There will be occasions when changes in availability or price force reconsiderations. Valid alternatives must then be sought. On other occasions institutional actions— budget cuts, freezes on purchases, or, sometimes, added funds—will require almost instant response. Librarians must be prepared for all such eventualities. They must know and understand the workings of the book world and of the financial world, since libraries function in both worlds.

Change is pandemic, but it is particularly hard for libraries, which depend on a certain level of stability, since most of their purchasing actions extend over a fair period of time and cannot readily be reversed. Librarians must be able to explain their working constraints in terms that others can understand. They may not always get the response they want or need, but having established good relations with budget makers and comptrollers makes success more likely. Involvement in long-term planning is essential, and to it librarians can bring, not only knowledge of their own needs, but a contextual knowledge that is useful to other planners. Use of the library, for example, reflects and foreshadows other changes and can be a helpful measure to evaluate the success of plans, or the likelihood of success in planned changes.

The Implications of Library Collecting

Above all, collection development and management is a long-term activity. Taking such a perspective will help librarians work their way through short-term perturbations. Over time any library's collections represent a major capital investment, one that in turn needs proper care to retain its value. Jack Dunn points out the importance of a managerial accounting concept—value maintenance—and its application to libraries.[12] The collection is at once an investment in the past and in the future, a salutary reminder to those who concentrate solely on the present that that present will soon be the past. Fads in learning, trends in management, crises in finance come and go, but the library's collections are a reminder that human wisdom is permanent, cumulative, and all-encompassing. What has been spent is not lost. It is still there, represented by the collections, and still earns its keep.

There are many questions of conservation and preservation involved, and these include the new electronic media as well as the older needs for mending and binding. Libraries require the same maintenance as other capital investments, and deferral of such needs can only raise their cost. Not all such expenditures are within the library materials budget, but that budget must deal adequately with such matters as repair, binding, replacement, substitution, withdrawal, and daily care. If such matters are neglected, the collections will deteriorate, and most published material simply cannot be readily replaced. An active binding and repair program is an essential part of the library materials budget, as is considered replacement, either by repurchase, reformatting, or purchase in another medium.

While all these matters cannot be covered exhaustively in a single volume, they must be kept in mind while reading the chapters that follow. This book is primarily concerned with financial matters, yet has to be based on goals and objectives. Budgets do not have a life of their own; their job is to help librarians carry out their policies. Not understanding how budgets work and the constraints inherent in any budgetary process can work against the achievement of any policy goals.

Notes

1. John A. Dunn, Jr., and Murray S. Martin, "The Whole Cost of Libraries," *Library Trends* 42,3 (Winter 1994): 574–76.

2. Association for Library Collections and Technical Services. Collection Management and Development Guidelines. No.1. *Guide to Writing a Bibliographer's Manual* (Chicago: 1987); No. 2. *Guide to the Evaluation of Library Collections* (Chicago: 1989); No. 3. *Guide to Written Collection Policy Statements* (Chicago: 1989); No. 4. *Guide to Budget Allocation for Information Resources* (Chicago: 1991); No. 5. *Guide to Review of Library Collections* (Chicago: 1991).

3. There are many articles on rising serials prices. Good general articles are: Stuart L. Frazier, "Impact of Periodical Price Escalation on Small and Medium-Sized Academic Libraries: A Survey," *Journal of Academic Librarianship* 18,3 (1992): 159–62; and Myoung Chang Wilson, "The Price of Serials Is Everybody's Business," *Bottom Line* 3,4 (1989): 12–14.

4. Jerry D. Campbell, "Academic Library Budgets: Changing the Sixty-Forty Split," *Library Administration & Management* 3 (1989): 77–79.

5. George R. Jaramillo, "Computer Technology and Its Impact on Collection Development," *Collection Management* 10,1/2 (1986): 1–13; Michael L. Nelson, "High Database Costs and Their Impact on Information Access: Is There a Solution?" *Journal of Academic Librarianship* 13 (1987): 158–62; David C. Taylor, "Serials Management: Issues and Recommendations," in *Issues in Library Management: Historical Perspectives and Current Reflections* (White Plains, N.Y.: Knowledge Industry Publications, 1989), 82–96.

6. *U.S. News and World Report* 113,12 (Sept. 28, 1992): 96–127. "What Must Be Done: Cutting Costs," 100–103, 110. "What College Presidents Think," 101.

7. Jim Traue, "Against the Grain," *New Zealand Libraries* 47,3 (Sept. 1992): 54–55. Cited in the article is Langdon Winner's *Autonomous Technology: Technics Out-of-Control as a Theme in Political Thought* (Cambridge: MIT Press, 1977).

8. R. Erickson, "*Choice* for Cooperative Collection Development," *Library Acquisitions: Practice and Theory* 16,1 (1992): 43–49; and Sue O. Medina, "The Evolution of Cooperative Collection Development in Alabama Academic Libraries," *College & Research Libraries* 53,1 (1992): 7–19.

9. Verner W. Clapp and Robert J. Jordan, "Quantitative Criteria for Adequacy of Academic Library Collections," *College & Research Libraries* 25 (1965): 371–80. *See also* Daniel W. Lester, "Twenty Years after Clapp-Jordan: A Review of Academic Library Funding Formulas," in *Financing Information Services: Problems, Changing Approaches, and New Opportunities for Academic and Research Libraries,* edited by Peter Spyers-Duran and Thomas W. Mann, Jr. (Westport, Conn.: Greenwood, 1988), 79–90.

10. Murray S. Martin, "The Implications for Acquisitions of Stagnant Budgets," *Acquisition Librarian* 2 (1989): 105–17.

11. Murray S. Martin, "The Invasion of the Library Materials Budget by Technology. Serials and Databases: Buying More with Less?" *Serials Review* 18,3 (1992): 7–17.

12. John C. Dunn, Jr., and Murray S. Martin, "The Whole Cost of Libraries," *Library Trends* 14,3 (Winter 1994): 564–78.

Chapter 2

Gathering Information for a Library Materials Budget Request

The quest for information begins with what you already know. The examination of existing records shows where you are now and gives a preview of the future. Since you usually begin preparing a budget request for the next year shortly after the beginning of the current fiscal year, the latest complete records will be for the previous fiscal year. The current year may also provide information about any trends in orders or price changes.

In a sense, the request is prepared as part of a three-year cycle, and information is often sought as to the library's requirements for a further year beyond the one that will be affected by the next budget. Trends and changes are therefore of vital importance when looking into the future. As Peter Drucker has properly remarked, "the only thing we know about the future is that it has not yet happened." We can only extrapolate from what we already know about the near past and what is happening currently. As he points out, planning is not a matter of determining the future but of making decisions now and seeing what effect they have as time goes by.[1]

Review of the Last Budget Year

If the fiscal year ends by July 1, by late August the records for the preceding year are usually complete. The same reasoning applies to other fiscal calendars. This delay is caused by the need to reconcile several sets of data to ensure the accuracy of the figures shown in the annual report. Examine this report carefully to determine whether the actual expenditure and its products in terms of purchases match the expectations with which the year began.

Table 2.1 sets out a hypothetical budget for a medium-sized academic library. This will be the basis for all budget modifications shown later in the book. This budget includes engineering as a special school. Music, art, business, or education could be so treated where one or more of those are a specialization. The reference allocation has been broken down by general academic area. It would therefore be possible to add these figures to the academic area totals to arrive at a full distribution. Binding could be broken down similarly, but would distribute approximately in line with the expenditures on serials. The "General" allocation includes allowances for interdisciplinary programs, for instance American Studies, Women's Studies, or Black Studies, which could, if necessary, be presented in a further breakdown.

As can readily be seen, serials account for 55 percent of the total, and, if standing orders for sets, annuals and the like are included, the total standing commitment is 62.5 percent. With a further 5 percent spent on binding, the budget flexibility is small. In addition, the expenditures on databases (for convenience placed in reference) really represent a standing commitment.

The distribution by academic area corresponds roughly with the institutional investment in each area, i.e., expenditures on salaries, supplies, and equipment. Because of recent rapid price increases, the sciences are using

TABLE 2.1   Library Materials Budget
Academic Library
Base Year

Area	Books	Standing Orders	Serials	Data-bases	Media	Micro-forms	Total	Percentage of Total
REFERENCE								
General	$ 3,000	$ 5,500	$14,000	$10,000	$ 1,000	$ 1,000	$ 34,500	3.45%
Fine Arts	2,000	2,000	9,000	3,000	1,000	—	17,000	1.70%
Humanities	4,000	6,000	15,000	9,000	—	—	34,000	3.40%
Science	5,000	8,000	19,000	10,000	—	—	42,000	4.20%
Social Science	3,000	3,000	5,000	7,000	—	—	18,000	1.80%
Technology	2,000	2,000	3,000	6,000	—	—	13,000	1.30%
Subtotal	19,000	26,500	65,000	45,000	2,000	1,000	158,500	15.85%
GENERAL								
Documents	8,000	—	3,000	—	—	2,000	13,000	1.30%
General	24,000	6,000	17,000	—	—	8,000	55,000	5.50%
Professional	2,000	1,000	2,000	—	—	—	5,000	0.50%
Replacements	10,000	—	—	—	—	—	10,000	1.00%
Subtotal	44,000	7,000	22,000	0	0	10,000	83,000	8.30%
FINE ARTS								
Art History	10,000	1,000	3,000	—	2,000	1,000	17,000	1.70%
Music	5,000	6,000	2,000	—	—	—	13,000	1.30%
Performing Arts	4,000	500	3,000	—	15,000	—	22,500	2.25%
Subtotal	19,000	7,500	8,000	0	17,000	1,000	52,500	5.25%
HUMANITIES								
Classics	5,000	1,000	3,000	—	—	—	9,000	0.90%
English	23,000	1,500	4,000	—	1,000	—	29,500	2.95%
Modern Languages	14,000	1,500	5,000	—	2,000	—	22,500	2.25%
Philosophy	8,000	300	5,000	—	—	—	13,300	1.33%
Subtotal	50,000	4,300	17,000	0	3,000	0	74,300	7.43%

(continued)

TABLE 2.1 *(continued)*

Area	Books	Standing Orders	Serials	Data-bases	Media	Micro-forms	Total	Percentage of Total
SCIENCE								
Biology	$ 6,000	$ 6,000	$ 80,000	$ —	$ 1,000	$ —	$ 93,000	9.30%
Chemistry	5,000	8,000	83,000	—	—	—	96,000	9.60%
Computer Science	3,000	1,000	6,000	—	—	—	10,000	1.00%
Mathematics	3,500	4,000	33,000	—	—	—	40,500	4.05%
Physics	3,600	2,000	80,000	—	—	—	85,600	8.56%
Subtotal	21,100	21,000	282,000	0	1,000	0	325,100	32.51%
SOCIAL SCIENCES								
Economics	9,000	700	11,000	—	—	—	20,700	2.07%
Education	6,000	1,000	10,000	—	2,500	1,500	21,000	2.10%
History	17,000	1,000	15,000	—	500	4,000	37,500	3.75%
Political Science	9,000	500	10,000	—	—	—	19,500	1.95%
Psychology	8,000	800	20,000	—	—	—	28,800	2.88%
Sociology	13,000	600	9,000	—	1,000	2,500	26,100	2.61%
Subtotal	62,000	4,600	75,000	0	4,000	8,000	153,600	15.36%
TECHNOLOGY (Engineering)								
General	2,000	500	11,000	—	1,000	—	14,500	1.45%
Chemical	2,000	500	13,000	—	—	—	15,500	1.55%
Civil	3,500	2,000	11,500	—	1,000	—	18,000	1.80%
Design	1,700	100	5,000	—	1,000	—	7,800	0.78%
Electrical	1,200	500	16,000	—	—	—	17,700	1.77%
Mechanical	4,000	500	25,000	—	—	—	29,500	2.95%
Subtotal	14,400	4,100	81,500	0	3,000	0	103,000	10.30%
BINDING							50,000	5.00%
GRAND TOTAL	229,500	75,000	550,500	45,000	30,000	20,000	1,000,000	100.00%
PERCENTAGE OF TOTAL	22.95%	7.50%	55.05%	4.50%	3.00%	2.00%	100.00%	

up an ever larger proportion of the whole (here 32.5 percent, as against 29 percent a year ago), and, if this trend continues, it will be necessary to consider dropping more subscriptions. Here the difficulty is the sciences' high level of serial dependence: 86.7 percent. In an institution with a high sci-tech presence, this is a continuing problem.

The library budget is now barely at the level of book buying that represents basic coverage, and any further erosion will make it hard for book-dependent disciplines to remain current. In the past, book expenditures in the sciences have been reduced to compensate for rising serial prices, but there is little room left to maneuver. If the parent institution is able to allow budgetary increases to compensate for inflation, the library should be able to continue the same level of support. If that turns out not to be the case, the librarians will have to make some hard choices between fields and types of publications. The database budget is a relatively new item, and the expectation is that it will grow, with more students and faculty relying on the direct purchase of articles. At this stage, it is still possible to provide free copies, but by next year there may have to be charges. These decisions are discussed in later chapters.

Table 2.2 sets out a comparable base budget for a public library. The basis for distribution here is the user, with provision for a general reference fund, since this serves many of the needs of the other areas. The business and career centers are new ventures, and a separate record is kept partly to provide information for grant seeking in the future, but also because it allows selectors to focus more clearly. The large print collection now needs to be supplemented by videos and audiotapes, and this adjustment will be made next year. There has been some question about the efficacy of the Young Adult collection, but use continues to be steady.

TABLE 2.2   Library Materials Budget
Public Library
Base Year

Area	Books	Standing Orders	Serials	Data-bases	Media	Total	Percentage of Total
REFERENCE	$ 12,000	$17,500	$ 4,500	$14,000	$ 500	$ 48,500	19.40%
ADULT							
Nonfiction	45,100	0	0	0	3,000	48,100	19.24%
Business (1)	4,000	2,000	3,000	2,000	1,000	12,000	4.80%
Careers (2)	2,000	500	2,000	2,000	500	7,000	2.80%
Periodicals	0	0	49,000	0	0	49,000	19.60%
Audiovisuals	0	0	0	0	10,000	10,000	4.00%
Gen. Fiction	31,000	0	0	0	0	31,000	12.40%
Mystery	2,600	0	0	0	0	2,600	1.04%
Romance	2,000	0	0	0	0	2,000	0.80%
Paperbacks	2,300	0	0	0	0	2,300	0.92%
Rental (3)	[6000]		0	0	0	[6000]	
Large Print	3,500	0	0	0	0	3,500	1.40%
Subtotal	92,500	2,500	54,000	4,000	14,500	167,500	67.00%
YOUNG ADULT							
Nonfiction	3,000	0	500	0	0	3,500	1.40%
Fiction	6,000	0	0	0	0	6,000	2.40%
Audiovisuals	0	0	0	0	4,000	4,000	1.60%
Subtotal	9,000	0	500	0	4,000	13,500	5.40%
CHILDREN							
Reference	2,500	0	1,000	2,000	0	5,500	2.20%
Nonfiction	3,000	0	0	0	0	3,000	1.20%
Fiction	5,000	0	0	0	0	5,000	2.00%
Picture Books	6,000	0	0	0	0	6,000	2.40%
Audiovisuals	0	0	0	0	1,000	1,000	0.40%
Subtotal	16,500	0	1,000	2,000	1,000	20,500	8.20%
GRAND TOTAL	130,000	20,000	60,000	20,000	20,000	250,000	100.00%
PERCENTAGE OF TOTAL	52.00%	8.00%	24.00%	8.00%	8.00%	100.00%	

Notes:
1. The Business Collection is supported by external grants.
2. The Careers Collection is supported partly by state funding and these funds would be lost if the library did not continue to provide a matching amount from its own budgetary resources.
3. The Rental Collection is self-supporting and is not included in the budget total.

The distribution by type of publication differs greatly from that for the academic library, with barely 24 percent of funds committed to serials. Again, databases are relatively new, and there are plans to extend the service, preferably through the local consortium. It would be advisable to provide a fairly simple breakdown of adult nonfiction, less by way of a classified structure (e.g., the Dewey classification) than by general interests, such as biography, self-help, gardening, cookery, history, and the like. The total amount to spend ($45,100) does not justify a complex breakdown, but some track should be kept of the kinds of materials purchased. The media center has been very successful, and there has been increasing demand for instructional as against entertainment materials; hence the allocations to various areas as well as a large central allocation.

These budgets will be used as examples throughout the book, with variations as appropriate.

Review of Performance

With any luck, by and large, the original intentions will have been met, but a cardinal rule in budgeting is that the end result seldom matches exactly the initial distribution. There are many reasons for such a difference.

Materials may not have been published either in the expected quantities or by the expected times.

Shipping, postal, or other strike action may have disrupted the normal flow of supply.

Prices may have increased more than allowed for in the original projection.

Any price increases were probably unevenly distributed and have had more impact on some areas than on others.

Unexpected vacancies, or other work pressures, may have reduced the output of selectors.

A special donation may have added to the workload and skewed the original distribution.

Unforeseen events may have increased the demand for replacements or duplicate copies.

Financial crises may have reduced or increased the original budget.

Any or all of these events may happen in any year, and the goal of the budget examination is to determine what effects they had and what, if any, corrective action needs to be taken. Look carefully at the differences between the original fund distribution and the actual expenditures. The year-end expenditures are shown in tables 2.3 and 2.4. Most of the differences came from price increases for serials and standing orders, but some arose from the differing habits of selectors.

The table for academic libraries shows that price increases for science and technology exceeded estimates. The final result is an overexpenditure of $25,850 (2.9 percent). The deficit was made up from salary savings and other underexpenditures. The message, however, is clear. Next year there will have to be serial cancellations and probably reductions in other expenditures as well. Book expenditures were held back but did not balance out other

TABLE 2.3   Library Materials Budget
Academic Library
Year-End Expenditure

Area	Books	Standing Orders	Serials	Data-bases	Media	Micro-forms	Total	Percentage of Total
REFERENCE								
General	$ 2,940	$ 5,210	$ 13,820	$ 9,760	$ 990	$ 1,110	$ 33,830	3.30%
Fine Arts	1,680	2,060	8,670	2,310	990	—	15,710	1.53%
Humanities	3,980	7,120	14,920	8,330	—	—	34,350	3.35%
Science	6,210	6,970	21,710	8,970	—	—	43,860	4.28%
Social Science	2,300	3,310	4,970	7,640	—	—	18,220	1.78%
Technology	1,610	2,520	3,210	5,900	—	—	13,240	1.29%
Subtotal	18,720	27,190	67,300	42,910	1,980	1,110	159,210	15.53%
GENERAL								
Documents	7,620	—	2,980	—	—	1,760	12,360	1.21%
General	21,310	7,590	18,620	—	—	9,000	56,520	5.51%
Professional	1,640	1,210	2,100	—	—	—	4,950	0.48%
Replacements	9,010	—	—	—	—	—	9,010	0.88%
Subtotal	39,580	8,800	23,700	0	0	10,760	82,840	8.08%
FINE ARTS								
Art History	11,250	750	3,210	—	2,310	1,550	19,070	1.86%
Music	5,210	6,910	2,050	—	—	—	14,170	1.38%
Performing Arts	3,250	210	2,910	—	17,620	—	23,990	2.34%
Subtotal	19,710	7,870	8,170	0	19,930	1,550	57,230	5.58%
HUMANITIES								
Classics	4,790	840	2,960	—	—	—	8,590	0.84%
English	23,920	1,260	4,010	—	940	—	30,130	2.94%
Modern Languages	14,260	1,600	5,720	—	2,160	—	23,740	2.32%
Philosophy	7,250	270	4,900	—	—	—	12,420	1.21%
Subtotal	50,220	3,970	17,590	0	3,100	0	74,880	7.30%
SCIENCE								
Biology	5,760	6,120	82,100	—	950	—	94,930	9.26%
Chemistry	6,120	9,010	85,650	—	—	—	100,780	9.83%
Computer Science	2,900	1,250	7,000	—	—	—	11,150	1.09%
Mathematics	3,750	4,760	34,710	—	—	—	43,220	4.22%
Physics	3,200	2,510	83,500	—	—	—	89,210	8.70%
Subtotal	21,730	23,650	292,960	0	950	0	339,290	33.10%
SOCIAL SCIENCES								
Economics	8,050	750	11,360	—	—	—	20,160	1.97%
Education	5,100	870	9,290	—	2,610	1,450	19,320	1.88%
History	16,700	990	14,910	—	490	3,960	37,050	3.61%
Political Science	8,650	320	11,200	—	—	—	20,170	1.97%
Psychology	8,210	910	22,500	—	—	—	31,620	3.08%
Sociology	11,350	620	8,900	—	970	2,800	24,640	2.40%
Subtotal	58,060	4,460	78,160	0	4,070	8,210	152,960	14.92%

(continued)

TABLE 2.3   *(continued)*

Area	Books	Standing Orders	Serials	Data-bases	Media	Micro-forms	Total	Percentage of Total
TECHNOLOGY (Engineering)								
General	$ 1,960	$ 610	$ 11,600	$ —	$ 970	$ —	$ 15,140	1.48%
Chemical	2,020	320	14,210	—	—	—	16,550	1.61%
Civil	3,600	1,650	12,100	—	960	—	18,310	1.79%
Design	1,650	120	5,010	—	820	—	7,600	0.74%
Electrical	1,300	610	17,260	—	—	—	19,170	1.87%
Mechanical	4,150	700	27,000	—	—	—	31,850	3.11%
Subtotal	14,680	4,010	87,180	0	2,750	0	108,620	10.60%
BINDING	—	—	—	—	—	—	50,100	4.89%
GRAND TOTAL	222,700	79,950	575,060	42,910	32,780	21,630	1,025,130	100.00%
PERCENTAGE OF TOTAL	21.72%	7.80%	56.10%	4.19%	3.20%	2.11%	100.00%	
Over/Under Expenditure	−6,800	4,950	24,560	−2,090	2,780	1,630	25,130	

increases. In the case of the public library, the same conditions obtained, but severe restraint in book expenditures reduced the deficit. The Business Center proved to be more expensive than had been anticipated, but it was heavily used and will be maintained.

Encumbrances

One vital difference may have been that requests came in late in one or more areas, and there may be substantial year-end encumbrances in those areas. Encumbrances represent the cost of orders that have been placed but not yet received. In due course they will be received and then will have to be paid for. How such encumbrances are treated in the ensuing year will depend on the budgetary style of the institution.

If it operates on an accrual basis, which means that activities are related to the fiscal year in which they take place rather than to the year in which money actually changes hands, any orders will have been encumbered against funds held from the year the encumbrance was made. The corollary is that the unexpended funds must be held in escrow until payment is made. Usually there is a time limit placed on such expenditures, and some outstanding orders may have to be cancelled or charged against the current year. A good explanation of the effects of accrual accounting is available in an article by Nancy Stanley.[2]

A more common practice is to use a cash basis, which is more realistic for continuous-flow activities such as ordering. This means that transactions are recorded as they take place, regardless of the fiscal year in which they occur. Any other practice would force the library either to adopt an order year, predating the fiscal year, or to cease ordering towards the end of each year.

TABLE 2.4 Library Materials Budget
Public Library
Year-End Expenditure

Area	Books	Standing Orders	Serials	Data-bases	Media	Total	Percentage of Total
REFERENCE	$ 13,000	$17,800	$ 5,000	$13,700	$ 400	$ 49,900	19.63%
ADULT							
Nonfiction	44,200	0	0	0	2,600	46,800	18.41%
Business	4,000	2,500	3,200	3,000	1,200	13,900	5.47%
Careers	2,000	450	1,900	1,900	700	6,950	2.73%
Periodicals	0	0	52,200	0	0	52,200	20.54%
Audiovisuals	0	0	0	0	11,000	11,000	4.33%
Gen. Fiction	30,000	0	0	0	0	30,000	11.80%
Mystery	2,400	0	0	0	0	2,400	0.94%
Romance	1,600	0	0	0	0	1,600	0.63%
Paperbacks	2,000	0	0	0	0	2,000	0.79%
Rental	[6,500]		0	0	0	[6,500]	
Large Print	3,400	0	0	0	0	3,400	1.34%
Subtotal	89,600	2,950	57,300	4,900	15,500	170,250	66.99%
YOUNG ADULT							
Nonfiction	3,100	0	500	0	0	3,600	1.42%
Fiction	6,000	0	0	0	0	6,000	2.36%
Audiovisuals	0	0	0	0	3,900	3,900	1.53%
Subtotal	9,100	0	500	0	3,900	13,500	5.31%
CHILDREN							
Reference	2,200	0	1,100	1,800	0	5,100	2.01%
Nonfiction	3,100	0	0	0	0	3,100	1.22%
Fiction	5,000	0	0	0	0	5,000	1.97%
Picture Books	6,100	0	0	0	0	6,100	2.40%
Audiovisuals	0	0	0	0	1,200	1,200	0.47%
Subtotal	16,400	0	1,100	1,800	1,200	20,500	8.07%
GRAND TOTAL	128,100	20,750	63,900	20,400	21,000	254,150	100.00%
PERCENTAGE OF TOTAL	50.40%	8.16%	25.14%	8.03%	8.26%	100.00%	
Over/under Expenditure	−1,900	750	3,900	400	1,000	4,150	

Because orders are placed continuously, reflecting publishing practice, there is likely to be each year a corresponding inflow of received materials. Some institutions insist on the cancellation of all outstanding orders at the end of each year, which may leave a library with substantial unexpended funds. Institutional practice must be taken into consideration when examining encumbrances.

The more important point here is to determine the distribution of encumbrances among the various allocations. If some allocations are very highly encumbered, with little expenditure, it may be necessary either to reexamine internal procedures or to reevaluate vendor performance. If there is a substantial overencumbrance along with substantial expenditures, there is a need to rethink both the allocation and the methods of control used.

Where there are few encumbrances and also few payments, there may be reason to think the original allocation was too high. The actual records of materials received may provide part of the answer. For example, a very expensive set may have been published which was also a high priority for the library, or such a planned publication may have been postponed or cancelled. In other cases, the records may show that delays in selection were caused by changes in program. These kinds of facts can then be taken into account in planning for the future. More will be said of these situations when examining budgetary control.

Other Records

The expenditure figures alone will not reveal all that is necessary to know. They can tell you how nearly expenditure matched fund allocation, and the gross amounts paid for various categories of materials, but they cannot tell you what was bought.[3] Acquisition records will show how many items of each format were ordered and paid for, but their classified distribution cannot be known until after cataloging has been completed. This may not always matter, if all that is needed is to know how many films or records were purchased, or if a fund corresponds with a specific library or department, but for proper analysis of the results it is necessary to know whether the collections grew in the manner expected.[4] By using the information from cataloging, it is possible to determine better whether the growth in collections corresponded with the original intention. In some settings it is also important to determine whether purchases corresponded with demand. Circulation figures can show whether or not there is a correspondence. Figure 2.1 shows these kinds of figures adapted to a common denominator, the classification system used. In this case it is possible to see that added volumes—those bought last year—are helping to adapt the total collection to actual usage patterns.

Because this is a title count only, it does not include bound volumes of periodicals. This kind of count may, to a certain extent, understate the science/technology collections (Q-T) and appears to overstate language and literature (P), though, since literature is a retentive discipline, as a proportion of the total collection it will always be high.

Certain areas show a use rate much higher than their proportion of the total collection. Here we see, for example, increased interest in non–U.S. History (D) and a growth in social concerns (HM-HX) and in health (R). Some segments of the collection are virtually noncirculating—e.g.; law (K) and reference and bibliography (Z)—while there is little interest at all in agriculture (S). Response to user interest changes is shown by increased current purchasing—(D, HM-HX, R)—offset, to some extent, by a decrease in literature (P). The apparent mismatch in economics (H-HJ) reflects the purchase of a multivolume set, which was cataloged as separates. Explanations for such an apparent discrepancy should always be sought. Current use patterns suggest a need for further expansion in philosophy (B-BJ), music (M), and fine arts (N). Another necessary activity is to examine in-house use

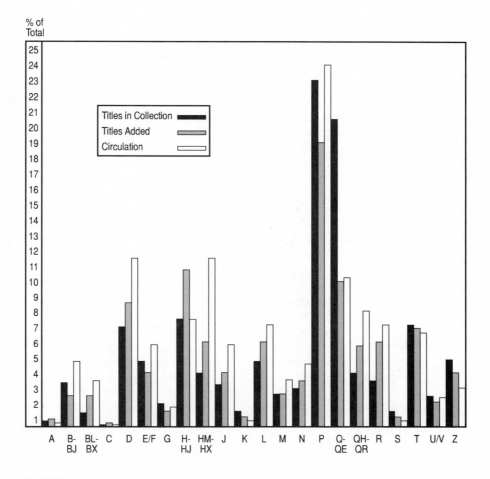

FIGURE 2.1   Collection and Usage Profiles

in primarily noncirculating areas. Reshelving figures for reference suggest continuing heavy use of all noncirculating reference materials.

A finer analysis also shows intense use in narrower classifications. For example, the theater and film collection within PN was being used to the point of destruction, thus indicating the need for a substantial replacement and repair program. Within the larger classification of literature itself, American literature (PS) continued to predominate in use, with British literature (PR) a close second. However, French and Spanish literatures (PQ) showed a resurgence, while Russian and German literatures diminished. Within non–U.S. history (D), the greatest growth was, in descending order, in histories of southern Africa, the Middle East, and Asia, with Europe remaining relatively steady, and use of the remainder almost nonexistent. While caution must always be exercised in interpreting such figures, and libraries must maintain a basic collection in all areas, these figures certainly suggest the appropriate intensities of collecting for this library.

The Current Year

When you have gathered as much information as possible about the last completed year, it is time to look for the same indicators in the current year. Here the need is to be sure that you are at approximately the same place in the fiscal year in terms of orders placed, received, and paid for. Comparisons may then be made by general budget expenditure, by format, or by specific subject allocation. In particular, if the first major payment for serials renewals has already been made (in August/October in most cases), it is also possible to tell whether there have been any substantial price increases, and whether these match or exceed earlier estimates. Their distribution will also be important in making future projections.

What are the differences between planned and actual acquisitions? Though these will vary from library to library, some general facts should emerge. Some categories of expenditure may show higher increases than others. These may relate to differential price increases if the acquisition rate remained relatively the same. On the other hand, a new emphasis or the need to improve some segment of the collection may have led to higher allocations and higher expenditures. If there were such planned changes, you should determine whether selection and purchase followed through on the plans. If so, then it may not be necessary to continue the same allocation pattern, since the immediate need may have been met, and so you can turn your attention to another area for enrichment. If not, then compensatory changes are in order. Most likely there will be a mix of both results. High rates of price increase may have pushed some sectors of the budget out of line, and reductions may be necessary to sustain other purchases. If the area or program is vital to the institution, reductions may have an adverse effect on users, and it may be necessary to ask for more money to cover the difference. More likely in poor economic conditions may be the need to reexamine long-term commitments such as serials to lower their proportion of the total budget and leave some room for other kinds of purchases.

Price Indexes

There are several aids to help in an examination of trends and results. Price indexes for many materials are published annually. *Library Journal* carries periodical and serial price increases; *Publishers Weekly* offers a range of book price indexes; *Microform Review* carries microform price information.[5] *Choice* each year presents a college-related review of both materials and prices, and several vendors provide either general or customized information. Incidentally, the *Choice* article also provides a rough estimate of the total book budget required by the average college library. Examination of the figures, allowing for items that are out of scope or not recommended, suggests that a minimum budget of $250,000–$300,000 is required.[6] A few other studies are available.[7] Several serial vendors publish not only retrospective surveys but projections of price increases.[8] These have the advantage of being based on library purchasing history and so provide a better base than wider ranging reports.

The Library Constituency

In planning any acquisitions budget it is important to keep people in mind. Libraries exist to serve the needs of a constituency. Keeping track of changes in that constituency is an essential part of planning. College libraries serve faculty and students, who are combined through a mix of academic programs. Knowing that mix, both the constituent parts and the importance of each, helps a library determine its collecting goals. Similarly, knowledge of the respective emphases placed on research and teaching can help determine the depth and the breadth of coverage needed.

Public libraries also serve multiple constituencies, though the determining characteristics are different—adults, young people, children, the business community, local authors and researchers. Each of these groups has its own needs, and changes in the mix will result in a different collection-development plan. Special libraries may serve rigorously defined communities— doctors within a given range of specialties, lawyers with definable fields of interest, or a business or research corporation with a clearly defined scope of operations. At least those specializations are clear to the specialists but, in library terms, they interact or overlap or may be so separate as to require virtually separate libraries.

The needs of these constituencies define themselves in different ways. While a faculty member may be most interested in current disciplinary advances and want mostly up-to-date information, a student may need basic information to pass courses. Together, they may require significant expenditure on research journals, reserve books, or multiple copies of basic works. Research- and teaching-oriented departments require differing collections, and the importance of either will determine the kind of balance needed.

The adult members of a local community may have general interests in a wide range of fiction or general works, or there may be specific interest generated by the activities of local business or industry. There may be need for a career center, or simply for leisure reading. If there is a significant visually impaired or retired population, there may be demand for large-print books or for nonprint alternatives. A growth in the proportion of children or young people may require a library to direct more of its expenditure to those groups, where replacement costs are often higher. Changes in social customs may render some sections obsolete or require the addition of retrospective materials, for example increased emphasis on diet and health-related cookery.

The point behind these examples is to stress that keeping track of user needs and interests is essential in shaping collection development to useful ends. Doing so enables the librarian to make choices concerning the most important kinds of purchases, and to see that current collecting matches current need. It is possible to go too far in that direction, and any library must always be aware of the need to maintain a broad general collection.

Whether this is the core collection now often referred to in writing about colleges, or the representative collection for a public library,[9] any library should be sure that fashion and current interest do not divert funds from maintenance of a good general collection, which includes the reference collection that is the library's service core.

All needs are subject to change, and by keeping a finger on the community pulse, the librarian can detect changes as they occur rather than scrambling after the fact with out-of-print purchases and other retrospective buying.[10] Proactive selection may not always be possible but should be the aim. In public libraries, interest in literacy and diversity may prompt a wide revision of selection and acquisition practices. In an academic setting, new or revised programs call up new information needs. New contracts or research interests may similarly change the information needs of special libraries. In preparing for a new budget request, try to give these needs shape and seek some early estimate of likely costs.

Final Review

Finally, sit back and look carefully at the present level of acquisition. Determine whether there are use factors, actual or potential, which might be reason for a change in distribution; if so, decide how they should be implemented—gradually or at one time. So apparently simple a development as a shift in the demographic constitution of a town's population may suggest a wide variety of changes, depending on whether the population changes relate to age or ethnic factors. In an academic setting, the upgrading of some programs and the downgrading of others will suggest a similar shift in library emphases. Or the institution may be planning the introduction of new graduate programs, which require a totally different approach to collecting, and a new mix of access and ownership. A business or research corporation may be changing its basis of operation and will need entirely new kinds of information, as for instance a shifting of emphasis from defense to medical technology.

All these facts must be assembled and evaluated before it is possible to put together an appropriate budget request. This cannot be done at the drop of a hat; so pertinent information must be sought all the time and organized to enable actual budget preparation to begin at the time chosen by the parent institution.

Notes

1. Peter Drucker gives extensive attention to the nature of planning in "Long-Range Planning," *Technology, Management & Society* (New York: Harper, 1967), 129–48.

2. Nancy M. Stanley, "Accrual Accounting and Library Materials Acquisition," *Bottom Line* 7,2 (Fall 1993): 15–17.

3. Accompanying item records, usually supplied along with the budget summary, will report on invoices paid, but these are not arranged in any order related to subject. They have to be checked to ensure that invoices were accurately assigned, but that is another matter.

4. Items purchased and items cataloged do not coincide exactly each year. The lapse of time caused by the actual processing and cataloging works against that,

but, unless there are extreme variations year by year, acquisition and cataloging programs will be, by and large, consonant.

5. In summary, indexes which are presently maintained cover U.S. book publishing in several categories, the most important of which is the U.S. hardcover trade books index. Vitally important are those for U.S. periodicals and U.S. subscription services. Others cover microforms and some foreign countries.

   The indexes are available in *The Bowker Library Annual,* which groups all indexes together; *Publishers Weekly,* where, usually in February, the book price indexes for the previous year are published; *Library Journal,* where, in May or June, the latest periodical price indexes are published; and *Microform Review,* which covers microform indexes. These and more are also set out in *Guide to Budget Allocation for Information Resources* (Chicago: ALA, 1991). There is still some uncertainty as to the best way of using such indexes, but the general feeling is that they are the best indicators of long-term trends. (*See* "Book Price Indexes," *Library Resources & Technical Services* 20 [1978]: 97–98.)

6. For example, Donna Alsbury, "College Book Price Information, 1992," *Choice* 30,7 (1993): 1083–89.

7. For example, Troy V. Brazell, Jr., "Comparative Analysis: A Minimum Music Materials Budget for the University Library," *College & Research Libraries* 32 (1972): 110–20.

8. The Faxon Company produces each year *The Faxon Planning Report,* which projects future serial prices for the library market. Similarly Baker & Taylor produces *Academic and Research Book Price Report.* Other vendors produce similar reports.

9. Nancy Pearl and Craig Buthod, "Upgrading the 'McLibrary,'" *Library Journal* 117,17 (Oct. 15, 1992): 37–39, describe the experience of the Tulsa City-County Library.

10. The problem here is that short publishing runs and the effects of the *Thor Power Tool* decision on inventories reduce the ready availability of older published books, whether or not they are officially out of print. This is particularly true for university presses, where the average edition may have a print run of only 700–800 copies. Ordinary titles, of course, may be remaindered soon after publication if they are not selling to expectation, thus making the search for replacements more arduous. On the other hand, when hardback copies are remaindered after the publication of a paperback edition, libraries can pick up the former much more cheaply—a good time for replacement shopping.

Chapter 3

Preparing a Library Materials Budget Request

All budgets have to be based on existing information and informed guesses as to the future. The accuracy of both will determine how appropriate the request will be, how well it will be received, and how well the proposed budget will meet the next year's needs.

The first step is to review the information already gathered. This will include:

information on price increases in library materials;

any institutional allowance for inflation;

information on new programs needing library support;

the institutional rules governing budget requests;

information on special funds;

the distribution and total of held-over requests;

encumbrances for orders not yet received;

knowledge of want items from earlier years.

When this material has been set in order, a picture of the next year will begin to emerge. This picture should clarify strengths and weaknesses, sources of budget strain, and possible areas where the library effort can be decreased.

The most basic decision, how much to ask for, may be largely determined by earlier institutional actions. In times of shrinking or stagnant budgets, most officers responsible for preparing and approving budgets will already have been informed of any constraints via the documents distributed from the central budget office. These are usually based on total budget expectations, and may range from a request to hold the line to a request for a reduction, or sometimes an increase, within stated limits.

Typical requests include:

a general reduction in the base budget—usually expressed as a percentage, but sometimes as a dollar amount;

actions directed at specific segments of the budget, e.g., decisions on salary increases, or on specific line items, such as equipment or telecommunications;

decisions to move certain kinds of expenditures from a central budget to unit budgets, with or without the transfer of any funds;

specific allowances for inflation. Since these can also be accompanied by a general reduction in the base budget, the result can be a kind of two-steps-backward-one-step-forward dance. Although this may seem strange, the goal is to realign expenditures in keeping with budget constraints and yet be able to respond to differential inflation rates, even if at an overall lower level, because many units (the library is an example) have to continue purchasing materials, and any other course of action would mean a double reduction;

exempting library materials from the general reduction, though it must be remembered that even a level budget is, effectively, a reduction;[1]

targeting specific programs for reduction or elimination.

Although many of these directives may primarily affect areas other than library materials, their influence within the larger library budget has to be taken into account. This consideration is of particular importance when considering "access" alternatives. There are often occasions when "robbing Peter to pay Paul" makes sense within the larger context, but much decision making will depend on the degree of flexibility allowed to the library. When it is possible to make transfers between funds or lines, it is easier to respond to such changes.

Since serials play an important role, at least in academic and special libraries, basic decisions in this area will help determine the lines of the total budget. For this reason, serials and quasi serials will be discussed separately in another chapter. At this point in the process, however, it is necessary to determine whether

there will be a cancellation project, either the first or simply another in a succession of such budget control steps;

funds must be freed for new subscriptions, either to support new programs or to keep up to date with changes;

the present distribution should be maintained;

the present distribution should be altered as a reflection of other institutional changes.

These are advance decisions that will have to be worked out in detail at a later time, when the actual budget for next year is known.

Because of the complex process by which all institutional budgets are determined, any budget request prepared at this time can only be a first approximation. Nevertheless, it must be as complete and accurate as possible. It is the only evidence that will be available to those who must make budgetary decisions. Figures must never be fudged. That kind of manipulation will always come to light and will undermine the trust that has been built up with the budget officers.

Following is a checklist of items to be settled:

1. What kinds of outcomes are wanted? Here you must decide whether the mix of materials from last year represented a desirable distribution, both by total numbers and by subject or program. Keeping track of use, as suggested earlier in figure 2.1, can help determine outcomes, but it is also good to refer to broader goals. This kind of difference is at the core of the article by Pearl and Buthod cited on p. 19, note 9. There a conscious decision was made that collecting meant more than simply being sure that there were no waiting lines for best-sellers.

2. Are there new items to consider? Although this question may concern new or previously uncollected media—e.g., CD-ROMs, database services and the like—it also covers once-in-a-while purchases such as the replacement of a heavily used dictionary, a new edition of an encyclopedia, or a multiyear serial index. This is also the place to consider microform replacement of bound serials, or the purchase of a long-desired microform collection of art materials. Even though few such purchases are likely to be made each year, knowledge of one or more such items would lead to a more equitable distribution of funds. One formerly common practice was to set aside a reserve fund for such purchases, but, with budgets frequently down to bare bones, unusual acquisitions must be built in from the start.

3. Should other kinds of services be included? This may be the time to consider adding new allocations for access, e.g., fax services or courier services. These will become permanent budget items, and the decision has to be made whether to add money for them to the request or to reduce other existing programs.

4. Is dealer performance satisfactory? Though this may not seem, at first sight, to be a budget item, slow delivery could be the cause of unacceptably high year-end encumbrances, while too many orders returned marked "not available" may negate much planning. This may also be an appropriate time to review all dealer contracts, looking at both discount and service factors. It is appropriate to review the results of approval plans to determine whether the profiles should be changed or the scope reduced. Approval plans save time internally and help assure that wanted items are not overlooked, but they may also reduce the amount of free money for firm orders. Since any negotiations are likely to take several months, it is not too soon to begin the process so that new agreements will be in place for the next fiscal year.

5. Should any changes be made in binding and repair programs? Here you should examine the possibility of substituting microform for bound back issues, or perhaps the possibility that the library can rely on delivery services from elsewhere. Decisions on cancellations may reduce the need for binding. In the other direction, it may be urgent to restore some parts of the collection that cannot be replaced or to search for funds for the preservation of an important special collection. Whatever the decision, now is the time to make

budget provision. The amounts that are left out or included will have further effects on later budgets.

6. An important but often neglected corollary is to look at associated costs. These may include items as mundane as pencils and date due slips, more expensive items such as the costs of bibliographic utility services, and those as far-reaching as changes in staffing. The implementation of an automated system, or its updating, can be the cause of major shifts in expenditure—for example, paying for bar codes instead of circulation cards, electronic files instead of a Kardex, and, even more important, procedures requiring new skills and a new mix of staff.

7. Finally, although the results may not show up directly in the library materials budget, the effects of decisions in favor of access or purchase on demand should also be considered. If serial subscriptions are cut, or the level of collecting in a subject is lowered, the result will probably be an increase in interlibrary loan or other resource retrieval activities. Unless these are allowed for in the budget, the program will be jeopardized and sooner or later even more painful adjustments will be needed. Such post hoc adjustments are always more difficult than preplanned changes. It may make excellent sense to establish an "access" budget to cover such costs.[2]

Another kind of associated cost is the need for cabinets for microform sets, or workstations for CD-ROMs. Decisions should not be made unilaterally but by bringing together all those affected, so that other essential budget provisions can be made.

Running through a checklist of this nature will help ensure that no major items were overlooked. The next step is to complete a first run at a budget estimate. How this should be done will depend on the budgetary style of the institution.

Budget Styles

The commonest kinds of budget are line item, program or performance, and zero-base budgets. The line item budget is the simplest: each line in the budget equals the total of the expenditures for a specific category—e.g., library materials or telecommunications. A variation is to provide specific lines for subcategories—e.g., books, serials, microforms; or database costs, long distance, fax. Its merit is that it is the easiest way to keep track of expenditures. In fact, most other budgets are transformed into line item accounts for this purpose. Its weakness is that it separates allied expenditures, which may allow incongruencies that have to be corrected.

Program or performance budgets combine the various lines appropriate to a specific activity and allow an administrator a better handle on complete costs. They flow from statistical analyses and depend on the objectives set for each year. Here the major problem for libraries would be the definition of "program." Some institutions think of the library as a program in itself (rather like a department) and leave the library to make finer distinctions.

It is possible, for example, to define Technical Processes as a separate program and to include all library materials there. That begs the question of the relationship of those materials to other library activities. After all, they could as well be seen as the province of the Circulation Department, while the Reference Department program depends on the use of reference materials, and leaving them out would falsify the program costs.

Whatever the course taken, the buying of materials will not be decentralized, and it is necessary to bring together all library materials funds into one distribution in order to exercise the proper accounting control. The budgets used in this book represent this kind of approach: a unified library materials budget distributed programmatically.

Zero-base budgets expect that the entire budget will be reworked from the ground up each year. In fact, in most government and nonprofit organizations, complete budget reworking is almost never required, partly because of the enormous effort required, but mostly because the goals and objectives do not change dramatically from year to year. In academic institutions, customs such as tenure and agreements such as union contracts greatly limit the kinds of staff reassessment that can be made in any year, and these usually represent 70 to 80 percent of the total budget. New programs or extensive changes may, however, require a totally reworked budget, and the experiences of the early 1990s suggest that deeper rethinking of budget plans will be needed. Both program and zero-base budgets require more extensive justification than do line item budgets, including the presentation of "outputs," though it is common even for the latter to be asked to present a quasi-programmatic justification statement. There are many good books available on the various budgetary styles,[3] and these should be consulted for further information.

Preparation for Change

Librarians preparing budget requests should not rely solely on history and expect to continue business much as before. They should actively review what has been done and prepare for change.[4] As the institutions around them change, so must libraries. Change for libraries is gradual, not at a snail's pace, but governed by such factors as the time taken to fulfill orders, the impossibility of cutting off subscriptions tomorrow, and the relative stability of demand. A shift from ownership to access for a specific group of materials, for example, cannot take place within the space of a single year unless the decision is made to close the library down. Such a change requires careful advance planning and a major educational program to reduce unwanted side effects. If this is the direction in which the library chooses to advance, the library materials budget may well be the first element to reflect the decision, but the full effects of the decision may not show up for three or four years.

Participants in the Budget Process

In preparing any budget request, the preparer must be aware of who will read the proposal. Much if not all of the success of a budget request will depend on the care with which the information concerning facts and figures is assembled and articulated.[5]

Within the library those who review any budget request can be expected to be familiar with library terminology. Even so, it is wise to present fully the reasons why this amount and not another has been requested. Not all supporting information will be needed for the final version, but it must be available for use if needed. Carol Chamberlain has made a good case for the ways in which data available from automated systems can be used to support budgetary planning, with much less labor than needed with manual systems.[6] Automation has also increased the availability of data about circulation. This improved information should be used to demonstrate library performance.

Others involved in the budget process cannot be expected to be familiar with library terminology, and any supporting statements should be reviewed for clarity. Geoffrey Allen warns that "librarians are great compilers of statistical data, but exhibit poor abilities in its interpretation and use."[7] Do not burden any presentation with superfluous statistics. Keep firmly in mind that those who are reviewing the budget data are also reviewing many others' presentations and will want to see only cogent data that justify the request. That "we have always done it this way" cuts very little ice with administrators. The library materials budget should be firmly linked to institutional and library goals *and* show how the budget requested seeks to further those goals.

Nonlibrary players in the budget game are a varied crew. Most academic libraries have an advisory library committee. Its role may vary from providing general advice to more active managerial responsibilities, including the need to sign off on budgets.[8] In addition most members will have strong opinions which they will convey to their external constituencies. Whatever the role of the committee, it is better to have its members informed, particularly of problems with rising prices and falling budgets and of changes in library collecting policies that they may have to face. It is better to have advocates than adversaries. This is especially true when it becomes necessary to reduce serial subscriptions[9] or to cut back on retrospective purchases. Public library boards have much the same kinds of responsibilities. In addition there are financial committees, who may have a measure of responsibility in determining the library budget, and friends groups; both should be given advance information and primed about the reasons for the request.

The real question is, Who has the final say? Very few libraries are set up as self-governing entities. Even those that are have a governing board. There may even be some uncertainty about who has final financial control, the city, county, or township, or the Board of Trustees.[10] Usually there is a budget officer whose job it is to present all budget requests to a financial committee, along with a recommendation. The committee may have to make recommendations to a council, or to a president, but it is unlikely that a reasoned recommendation will be overthrown. The budget officer is a key player, and the librarian should seek to establish good relations with that officer. Such people usually want more detailed explanations and more data than committees. For the latter, extraneous details detract from the main task, that of deciding whether the general request is justified.

Notes

1. Murray S. Martin, "The Implications for Acquisitions of Stagnant Budgets," *Acquisition Librarian* 2 (1989): 105–17.

2. Public librarians in particular would benefit from reading *Creating a Financial Plan: A How-to-Do-It Manual for Librarians* by Betty J. Turock and Andrea Podolsky (New York: Neal-Schuman, 1992).

3. For a careful discussion of this topic, including whether it may become necessary for libraries to charge for access, three articles should be consulted: "Serials Management in the Age of Electronic Access" by Clifford A. Lynch, *Serials Review* 17,1 (1991): 7–12; "High Database Prices and Their Impact on Information Access: Is There a Solution?" by Michael L. Nelson, *Journal of Academic Librarianship* 13 (1987): 158–62; and "Serials Management: Issues and Recommendations" by David C. Taylor, *Issues in Library Management: A Reader for the Professional Librarian* (White Plains, N.Y.: Knowledge Industry Publications, 1984), 82–96. These articles provide a great deal of information for consideration. Further information is available in *Access versus Assets* by Barbra B. Higginbotham and Sally Bowdoin (Chicago: ALA, 1993).

4. Zero-base budgeting is fully covered in *Zero-Base Budgeting in Library Management: A Manual for Librarians* by Ching-Chih Chen (Phoenix, Ariz.: Oryx, 1980). Harold Chester Young's *Planning, Programming, Budgeting Systems in Academic Libraries* (Detroit: Gale, 1974) provides an overview of this approach.

5. Suggestions concerning budget preparation are more fully set out in *Academic Library Budgets* by Murray S. Martin. (Greenwich, Conn.: JAI Press, 1993). Although that book is primarily concerned with academic libraries, the same principles apply to all libraries.

6. Carol E. Chamberlain, "Fiscal Planning in Academic Libraries: The Role of Automated Acquisitions Systems," *Advances in Library Organization and Management* 4 (1986): 141–52.

7. Geoffrey G. Allen, "The Management Use of Library Statistics," *IFLA Journal* 11 (1985): 211.

8. Donna Packer, in "Acquisitions Allocation Equity: Politics and Formulas," *Journal of Academic Librarianship* 14 (1988): 276–86, refers to the adverse effects of a faculty takeover of the acquisitions budget.

9. More will be said in chapter 6. Paul Metz provides an excellent summary of the process in "Thirteen Steps to Avoiding Bad Luck in a Serials Cancellation Project," *Journal of Academic Librarianship* 18,2 (1992): 76–82.

10. The problems of the County of Erie Library Trustees and the County Government (noted in several successive news notes in *LJ Hotline* during 1992) suggest that there may be several ways of viewing budgetary authority. Although the trustees finally established their authority in this case, the same may not be true universally. For the reverse situation one may refer to the decision made by the Multnomah County Commissioners to discontinue free telephone reference service, despite the opposition of the librarian. It is highly desirable to have *all* influential people on your side.

Chapter 4

The Traditional Budget Process

In this chapter it is assumed that the library has received a request to present a budget without preset limits, constructed in accordance with acccompanying instructions. The library is expected to present a case for consideration by other officials.

Even though this may be the exception rather than the rule in the early 1990s, such a budget is nonetheless that against which all other budgets must be compared. It is the one which sets out the amount of money needed to permit the library to maintain its programs or even to expand to meet increased demand for its services. In order to present any other budget, there must be an understanding of what the full budget could have been and what it would have accomplished. Only then is it possible to see what changes (cuts or additions) will have to be made. This kind of examination also assists the librarian in planning the changes that may result from the budget eventually approved.

At the conclusion of the last chapter, a first draft of the new library materials budget was ready for library examination. During that examination the participants will have to reconcile internal, library priorities with external, institutional priorities. This is the stage during which issues relating to access and ownership have to be worked out. If the library, perhaps at institutional urging, is placing a greater emphasis on resource sharing and other cooperative programs, it is necessary to see how these goals relate to those of the collection development program.[1] If there is a drive to widen the outreach program, that may require rethinking of some materials categories, most specifically on-line access. If completion of an automation program has first priority, other investments may have to be held back for the time being. All such matters must be decided before completing the budget for presentation to any outside reviewers.

If, in the course of discussion, it appears that the original request must be modified, be prepared to rework the draft budget to mesh with other library needs. At the same time, be prepared to point out the effects those changes will have on the original program. The various constituencies within the library will also exert pressures to have the budget meet their goals—for example, more online access, more young adult services, or serials maintenance in a specific area. While these matters will have been considered in the course of preparing the preliminary budget, any new arguments advanced should be weighed against the effects of any changes in allocations.

Budget Projections

At this stage it is very important to incorporate all institutional requirements. While the actual monetary decisions being made will cover only the next fiscal year (except in institutions that must prepare a biennial budget), projections are usually required for the following year, or even for two years. While everyone realizes that firm projections are impossible, institutions must prepare long-term plans, and they need all the help they can get.

Fluctuations in library materials prices are particularly difficult to explain or predict. In this area dealers can and do supply information and can help with forecasting.[2] The budget instructions themselves may confuse the issue by providing an inflation allowance and requiring that the budget presented make no further such allowance. Sometimes they will set limits for increases unless added justification is provided but leave the nature of that justification up to the unit. Program changes elsewhere that affect the library may be decided without reference to the library; their results may have to be incorporated later. The instructions may ask that all changes be set out in detail as amendments to the base budget, in which case library budget officers must develop a common understanding of how they are to be determined. On the other hand, projections may be sought in broad outline only, based on a best guess as to the likely future. Occasionally, institutions, recognizing that the library is tied to certain suppliers in ways that other units are not, may make an allowance for foreign currency fluctuations, a kind of supplement to be drawn on if necessary.[3]

Often budget increase requests must be prioritized, a process that may require the consideration of multiple scenarios. Here the library must decide on the priority it will give to library materials and access. If it is the institutional practice to require numbered priorities (e.g., first, second, third), then placing library materials needs into one of these categories may result in quite different treatment, depending on how far down the priority list the institutional budget can reach. While it might appear that maintaining the collections would always be a first priority, it is easy to imagine a setting where automation or retrospective conversion might have a higher ranking. It is also possible to split priorities, placing, say, serials price increases before those for books, or putting new on-line resources first. All such decisions must be made in the light of likely funding.

If all first priorities are granted, but no third priorities, a library which placed library materials in the latter category would have severe difficulty in meeting the institution's information needs, and might have to ask for further exceptions when setting up the actual budget. Another kind of response could emphasize ownership less than access—e.g., funding for such programs as The Scholar's Express.[4] In that case, equipment, on-line services, and supporting personnel would be emphasized over actual materials, and the local community would have to be prepared for significant changes in the way the library responded to its information needs. All such activities are additional to the usual precautions taken to examine the effects of inflation and increased demand.

In making forecasts over any extended period, special attention has to be paid to long-term plans. As will be discussed more specifically in the chapter on serials, the long-term plan is the place to describe any planned serial adjustments. These may include general cancellations, holding the line on dollar expenditure, or more targeted projects, e.g., reducing the effects of high inflation in areas such as science.[5] Because there is a time lag in all such programs—cancellations take effect only after the end of the current subscription period—emphasis should be laid on the need for coordinated financial planning.

If the library is working to upgrade collection services in specific areas in response to community need, these should be described and emphasized. In particular, any need for substantial retrospective purchasing should be noted, stressing the time needed to complete such purchases. If overseas purchases are contemplated, reference should be made to currency fluctuations. Anticipated special payments, as for such cumulative indexes as *Chemical Abstracts,* should be mentioned if the sums involved are substantial. A program to substitute microforms for bound serials may also require sustained funding, not only for materials but for equipment, since the space and other savings cannot be recovered if the program is interrupted.

These examples are given to emphasize that justifications are needed for special expenditures. Most budget forms do not allow for extensive documentation, being intended for quick reading and easy comprehension. Because libraries represent a special budgetary case, supplementary statements are acceptable. Mostly these will be read only by budget officers and those responsible for advising the final decision makers. It is important to make a good case, referring not only to the expenditures involved but also to their role in the institution's programs.

Special Funds

If there are substantial special funds, these should be highlighted, along with the rules governing their use. In easier budget times this is usually not necessary, but when most institutions want to slow down or even arrest budgetary increases, it is important to ensure that special funds are not seen as a way of reducing other budgetary support.

Most endowed funds are accompanied by a statement of purpose. These may make it essential to confine acquisitions within narrow limits. If they are considerable, there is the danger that their use can distort allocation patterns unless regular funds are maintained.[6] In other circumstances, it may be necessary to delay expenditures until sufficient funds accumulate to buy needed but expensive items. Here the need is to explain that the funds are being retained for a reason. Sometimes the terms of a gift require that expenditure be only for collection enrichment, i.e., it may not substitute for other regular expenditures, even in an area that the library would ordinarily support substantially. The effects of these restrictions need to be explained in relation to the budget request.

The purposes of other funds may be more loosely defined. A National Endowment for the Humanities grant, which requires matching from local funds, is seldom intended only to provide additional purchasing power, but the general intention is to allow the library to *improve* its holdings in the designated areas. Here, the resulting problems are twofold. First, the funds can be used only in some areas, which may make it difficult to maintain balancing expenditures in other areas not similarly endowed. Second, budget officers may be tempted, in hard times, to see such funds as part of the regular budget, thus allowing them to keep other budgetary support lower, or even to reduce general funds allocated to the library. Actions of this sort not only undercut the purpose of the original grant but may also weaken the whole library program. This observation does not suggest a planned attack, only that saving money can become a very important budgetary goal. The librarian should be prepared to suggest ways in which special funds can be used to further both library and institutional goals, perhaps by showing how other allocations can be adjusted to reduce the distortions.

Allied Budget Areas

There are other allied budget areas which should not be overlooked. Any change in the purchasing program will have side effects. For instance, there may be increases or decreases in bibliographic utility costs, added or reduced personnel needs, changes in binding costs (which not only reflect changes in the numbers of serials but may also result from the substitution of paperbacks for hardbound books), bar codes for books, and maintenance for databases. While these may not be major budget items, inability to accommodate them may result in undesirable holdups in processing. Similarly, if the intention is to purchase major microform sets, steps must be taken to ensure that there are filing cabinets available. Change to access from ownership will increase costs in other operational areas, and special accounts may need to be set up to cover additional costs in those areas.

When the internal review has been completed, go over the budget request to make sure that nothing has been left out. In particular, check for internal consistency and correct tabulations. Make certain that supporting statements address the financial issues and conform to budget instructions. In addition, prepare arguments to support the request during external review.

External Review

External reviews take many forms but generally consist of three parts:

1. Inspection to see whether the request follows the instructions
2. Preliminary review by the budget office
3. Final review by the approving officer or committee.

The aims of each of these reviews are allied but different. Part one aims to ensure adherence to institutional policies and procedures—setting a level playing field. It is a technical review; hence the importance of following instructions exactly and submitting the request in the approved format. The library may be given the opportunity to correct any errors discovered, or they may simply be noted for later hearings.

The second part is usually an informal review that helps the budget officer to be sure of understanding the purpose and the details of the budget request. This is the time when additional supporting information can be brought forward. Since most budgets are set out in gross amounts, the various components should be explained. Evidence of projected price increases, currency fluctuations, and the like can be presented. Although not always explicitly requested, evidence of use can bolster a request. With program or performance budgets these factors are built into the instructions. Even so, it does not hurt to explain more fully what they mean.

Although anecdotal evidence usually is not considered strong, it may be useful to describe user response to new services, such as databases, to show that the expenditure was justified. Similarly, conversion of serial back runs to microform can be supported as a sensible use of space resulting in long-term savings. Such discussions can also elicit from the budget officer suggestions about adjustments, discussions of better ways to demonstrate need, or some advance indication of the likely institutional response.

The final review may or may not provide for a hearing. If it does, preparations should be made carefully. Prepared statements can be submitted (usually based on clues gathered during the review with the budget office), but, in general, what is required is a response to specific questions. These questions may seem marginal or even irrelevant—Why this many books, and not that many?—or partisan—Why are you cutting back on science books?—but they reflect personal concerns and cannot be brushed aside. After all, these are the people who will decide the library budget. These kinds of problems are easier to handle if the affected parts of the community have been involved in the budget process. Be as concise and to the point as possible, and avoid library jargon. Those concerned in the budget process at this level have little time for detail.

Budget Decision Making

Institutional decisions are not always based on how good a case was put for the specific year in question. Richard Talbot, in analyzing ARL library budget history, came to the conclusion that, for the most part, university administrators seem simply to have allocated the library a fixed percentage of the total budget.[7]

Ultimately, the decision depends on other knowledge, such as the likely income from taxes, state funds, or tuition. Growth or decline in these income sources determines the whole budget, and the share set aside for the library cannot endanger other priorities. Those other factors may include the need for added student financial assistance (usually a top priority); added general operational costs, such as heat, light, and power; or the effects of negotiated salary increases. They may also reflect an institutional commitment to upgrade some other component, such as the central computer-service unit. The result may be a final budget which does not reflect the library's own priorities. Its effect will depend on the degree of flexibility available to the library. If the decisions are made strictly by category, with some needs allowed and others disallowed, the library program can be seriously disrupted. Usually, however, the library is allowed some latitude to adjust its budget internally while staying within overall budget limits.

If it is part of the process, a concluding review with the budget officer can help explain any inconsistencies and determine what actions the library can take to improve matters in the course of budget implementation.

Notes

1. Wherever the term *collection development* is used in this book, the reference is to the library materials budget as the reflection of this policy. *Collection management,* on the other hand, is used to cover all activities relating to resource use, including resource sharing.

2. All would admit that forecasting library materials prices is not an exact science. Celia Wagner of Blackwell's (in "Book Prices, Publishing Output, and Budget Forecasting," *Against the Grain* 4, 5 [Nov. 1992]: 5–6), gives some reasons why this is so, and also some valuable suggestions for libraries that need to forecast expenditures. In the same issue, Phil Greene of EBSCO begins the column "Mourning Serial" with an examination of the past year's decline in the value of the dollar.

3. Fred Lynden, in a presentation at the 1992 Charleston Conference, said that Brown University had been willing to set up a currency adjustment fund.

4. Director Sharon Rogers of George Washington University Libraries, at the 1992 Spring Conference of the New England Chapter of the Association of College and Research Libraries, described in detail the process by which the university transferred funds from cancelled subscriptions to a fund designed to enable faculty to obtain articles from other sources.

5. For example, Princeton University Libraries Director Donald Koepp persuaded the faculty to agree to holding steady the total dollar amount to be spent for serials from certain European dealers. There are numerous accounts of similar actions designed to maintain some flexibility within the library materials budget.

6. An illustrative example is the receipt by the Greenwich (Conn.) Public Library of a very substantial endowment intended for the purchase of music records and business materials at a time when the library was facing major budget cuts.

7. Richard J. Talbot, "Financing the Academic Library," in *Priorities for Academic Libraries,* edited by Thomas J. Galvin and Beverly P. Lynch (San Francisco: Jossey-Bass, 1982), 31–44. A more recent survey of twenty-four ARL libraries, sponsored by the Andrew W. Mellon Foundation, indicated that the percentage, after being relatively stable for a number of years, has now fallen to its lowest level since 1968. This has not usually meant an actual decline in total budgets but simply reflects the fact that other items of expenditure have been rising more quickly or seem to have more importance to administrators.

Chapter 5

Other Budget Scenarios

The previous chapter addressed the traditional kind of budget process, in which units are asked simply to prepare budget requests based on need. It is more common for some kinds of restrictions to be placed on requests. In addition to the no-increase budget, which is actually a variation on the budget decrease, these may take a variety of forms:

A set percentage allowed for inflation (**steady state**)

A set percentage total increase (**controlled growth**)

Targeted increases, e.g., no added positions but more money for library materials (**selected growth**)

A set percentage total decrease (**overall reductions**)

Targeted decreases, e.g., reductions in positions, decreases in support expenditure, steady or reduced library materials budgets (**selected reductions**)

The targets may also be expressed in dollars. The various restrictions can be combined. For instance there may be an allowance for inflation but a prohibition against adding to the base budget. Here a case can be made for a higher inflation allowance for library materials, since this can be documented, but not for money to buy more materials. The various scenarios will be described briefly and their effects on the library materials budget analyzed.

The various budget expectations require radically different responses *if* the library is to attempt to maintain its programs. Unlike most institutional purchasing, the key to good collection management is a relatively steady budget. For one thing, the supply of new materials is relatively constant, and books, unlike supply items, are not interchangeable. Their purchasing is a continuous operation, unamenable to being turned on and off without severe consequences. Substitutes for books not purchased are not readily available at a later date, since many titles go out of print quickly. The same kind of continuity is essential for other materials. Electronic databases must be kept current, and an incomplete set of a microform project will simply cause frustration.

Steady State

A pre-set inflation allowance, which is usually based on the cost of living and similar indexes, often understates price inflation for library materials.[1] One regular index that can be used effectively is the Higher Education Price Index,[2] which has a separate indicator for library materials. It may be possible to persuade the parent institution to provide a special allowance, but this is an unlikely gambit.

If the transfer of money between budget or program lines is allowed, it may be possible to transfer money to library materials. This maneuver can be useful if the general inflation allowance covers more than the anticipated expenditures in other budget categories, i.e., it is possible to reduce some expenditures and still meet actual need. This strategy is likely to be a one-time move, however, since other budget elements cannot be reduced substantially without affecting library services. Unless it is possible to make up the entire difference, it will be necessary to reduce library materials purchases. Transferring relatively small amounts of money simply delays major decisions without enabling the library to maintain the same level of purchasing. Because price increases are differential, no matter what savings can be made elsewhere, the allocation pattern will change. The basic decision, therefore, is where the cuts will be made. The most likely result is that there will have to be substantial cuts in the areas showing the highest rates of increase.

Set Budget Increase

A pre-set total budget increase leaves open the option of rearranging internal allocations. Other factors then come into play. Unless salaries are handled separately, any provision for salary increases usually has precedence and may require a substantial proportion of the total increase. Inflation also affects other budget areas, including telephone services, postage, and supplies. Here a careful examination of future needs may suggest possible reductions, but the amount involved is likely to be relatively small. The library may decide that, in order to free up money for materials, the hours of opening should be reduced. Although this strategy appears to offer substantial savings, the savings may not be worth the public aggravation. The likeliest savings, unless it is possible to reduce permanent staff, would be in wage or part-time positions, although even these are unlikely to yield significant transferable savings. Although some public libraries have reported that staff have been willing to forgo salary increases in order to maintain collections, such moves have drawn as much opposition as support. Basically, therefore, the library must decide whether to maintain collections or services. Some compromise position can be found, but arriving there may take longer than is available to prepare the actual budget. Adjustments are most likely to take place when the final budget is being set up.

Targeted Increases

Sometimes budget increases will be targeted. Apart from already negotiated salary increases,[3] the most likely object of such a program would be library materials. Here, the side effects can be substantial, in processing costs or even staff time if the increase is beyond inflation. The most likely situation is some increased allowance for inflation, or a special allowance for foreign currency fluctuations. Whatever the actual increase, the intention is clear. This is the budget area to be emphasized. Collection growth is to be maintained, even if other services are to be reduced. The result will be a shift in the percentage of the budget allocated to library materials. To some extent this reflects the thinking of many librarians, who have been disturbed by the continuing erosion in library buying power. While this is in some ways an admirable attitude, it depends for success on greatly increased staff productivity, since a library's collections are only as accessible and useful as the staff can make them. Suggestions have been made that cataloging standards can be lowered to save costs.[4] While this may have superficial appeal, the result is likely to be a lowering of accessibility, particularly in an automated environment where it is essential that all records be compatible. Once again it is clear that the full consequences of any budget decision must be understood.

Some, notably Richard Abel,[5] have argued that it is time for libraries to reconsider the priority given to serials. He believes that libraries should reemphasize books, at least partly because their unit price is lower and their potential readership is higher, but mostly because many of the high-priced serials are simply vehicles of record and are not truly used to disseminate new knowledge. It is true that many book collections have become tenuous and that coverage has been reduced as libraries seek to concentrate their expenditures. The problem is that this attitude implies that all serials and all books are alike. Many serials, particularly those in the humanities and the social sciences, convey much more than data and may be the only source for knowledge as well as information.

Too many libraries have reduced "marginal" serials which are at the cutting edge of their disciplines in favor of older, well-established serials which often reflect outmoded scholarly approaches to their subject matter. Nowhere is this more true than in literary studies, where "little magazines" usually provide guidance to new directions. The problem is one of balancing quantity and quality. Under a selective growth scenario, many disciplines will be shortchanged unless the library is willing to make radical revisions in collecting policy.

Overall Decrease

It is quite common for institutions to ask for an overall budget decrease, which reflects a similar decrease in income sources. Decreases may be relatively small or as large as 30 to 40 percent. Moreover, especially for public libraries, they may result from drastic cuts in specific funding sources for which no alternatives are available. There may or may not be specific directives as to how this decrease should be managed. Generally, some flexibility is allowed, although sometimes different parts of the budget are subject to different levels of reduction. Since the directives are general, libraries have to decide where and how to make the specific cuts. Staff agreements (tenure, for example, or union contracts) may dictate the limits of the responses available within the total budget. They may also dictate the kinds of changes that can be made. Here libraries can examine vacant positions, but, when the cut is large, staff may have to be laid off. Where these cuts occur may affect the library materials budget, in that processing costs must remain in some way consonant with the inflow of materials. Also, if the library is seeking to implement access programs, these must be adequately staffed. Operating expenditures are a frequent target, though here "free" funds relate mostly to travel and training or to equipment purchases. Reductions elsewhere—telecommunications, automation, supplies—have direct programmatic effects, and expenditures must be kept at the level necessary for daily operations. In any case, savings from this portion of the budget are likely to be small.

These facts leave only library materials to absorb the reduction, and this "funnelling" effect actually magnifies the results of the cut. Most libraries have tried at least to maintain basic purchasing power, but nearly all have been forced to reduce expenditures on library materials. Even where budgets appear to have increased, closer examination will show that the increases have not kept pace with inflation. In an attempt to cope, more and more libraries have begun to seek gifts and grants for library materials. There is a limit to how far this process can extend, since there are many other libraries competing for such largesse. Most institutions also have priorities for grants and gifts which are not always library related.

Targeted Decrease

Targeted decreases may make budget cutting easier, in the sense that some major decisions have already been made. On the other hand, such cuts may simultaneously serve to distort the library's programs unless they have been made in an informed manner. The need is to control budgetary strategies in accordance with some overall plan.

The usual perception is that administrative overhead and optional expenditures have gotten out of hand. Besides, the library tends to be regarded as overhead (or, in the public library setting, as a luxury). The aim may therefore be to reduce the whole library budget. Any effort to respond will underline the importance of relating library inputs and outputs to those of other programs in the case of academic and special libraries, or to general community needs in the case of public and school libraries.

The general inclination is to regard travel, memberships, and training expenditures as dispensable when, in fact, the library staff needs continuing exposure to the rapid changes in library and information technology. Also widely held is the belief that paper-based technologies are destined to be replaced quickly by machine-based technologies. No consideration is given to the costs of conversion, nor to the fact that for many purposes paper will continue to be indispensable. While this attitude may result in a willingness to finance automation, it ignores the fact that the majority of local information needs are, and will continue to be, met by paper, notably books and periodicals. There are settings where electronic information is becoming dominant, but these are, at least at the time of writing, in highly selective areas. The library, faced with mandated cuts, must seek to determine how much of the essential information base can be maintained, and what areas can be cut back without affecting too greatly the information needs of those served. This process, which can be called selective reduction, transfers responsibility directly to the library in determining whose needs will be sacrificed.

Disguised Budget Decrease

There is also a disguised budget decrease. This tends to occur when salary increases are kept outside the negotiation process. If those increases equal or exceed any allowance for inflation, other segments of the budget which did not benefit from similar allowances will be depressed, even though the whole budget appears to have increased. This kind of process diminishes the library's ability to shift funds within the budget. The result may be a budget which gives the appearance of health but which, in fact, diminishes the library's purchasing power. In such a situation, it is virtually certain that the library will have to decrease the purchase of library materials.

Library Responses

The only kind of budget which allows a library to maintain all its collections and services is one which makes full allowance for inflation (i.e., in everything from salaries to book prices). Even such a budget makes no allowance for new needs or new programs; if they are to be financed, they must be supported at the expense of existing programs.

In this setting the librarian is relatively free to determine the library's destiny. Even so, the costs of doing business as usual are disguised. Annual budgets seldom make provision for the full costs of housing the collection. In a major research library the addition of fifty thousand new volumes in a year requires more than a mile of new shelving, and the latter figure can be reduced only if some compensatory withdrawals are made. Long-term costs for additions, renovations, or new buildings are hidden by current budget procedures and addressed only when there is a crisis, usually long after the first steps should have been taken. Libraries must be aware of such needs. They may, as much as any others, play a role in collection development. It is folly to continue loading stacks that are already overfull, and remote storage may cost as much as new construction.[6] The alternative may be a massive weeding program, which also costs money, and which may weaken the collection unless handled carefully. Conversion to microformat or electronic files can save space but also costs significant sums of money which have be built into the budget. Setting aside funds for conversion on a regular basis may be prudent, even in times when budget constraints are minimal.

Making Budget Cuts

In most circumstances the library must decide where to make cuts. There are three ways in which this can be done. If the allowance for inflation is less than the predicted increase in prices, the library can elect to

1. increase all allocations by the inflation differential allowed;
2. retain the same percentage distribution within the library materials budget;
3. recalculate allocations to maintain the same percentage distribution that would have resulted from maintaining the full purchasing program.

All three alternatives presume that the existing allocations are in line with actual need. These alternatives are set out in table 5.1 for an academic library. It is also possible to alter allocations to redistribute funds in accordance with new needs, but this is simply a variation on the three principal modes set out above.

Because all their implications may not be immediately self-evident, the three processes are described below.

1. All allocations are increased by the allowance made for inflation. While this solution may seem, at first glance, equitable, clearly it will affect adversely those allocations facing an unusually high rate of inflation. Buying power will be sustained for those with lower rates of increase but significantly reduced for those with higher rates. In some circumstances—for example, when the decision has been made that such reductions are necessary to maintain general purchasing power—this procedure can be used.

2. The same percentage distribution is maintained within the library materials budget. Even if the original distribution represented the ideal, those areas with the highest rate of inflation will still be penalized. In certain settings this would be acceptable—for instance, if those areas were not of primary importance. Since they are likely to be in the science-technology-medical areas, this qualification is unlikely to be met.

3. Recalculating the allocation to reflect the distribution that would have been required to maintain all purchases. While this may seem a complex approach, it maintains something like the original distribution and also distributes the "pain" more evenly. Undoubtedly all areas will have to take cuts. Those affected by high inflation rates will not be unduly penalized, and those with lower inflation rates will not have to bear the whole burden.

The third method appears to this author the most equitable and the most readily justifiable.

A fourth alternative, which eliminates some areas or reduces them drastically, is available, but it depends on other administrative decisions as to the importance of the programs in question. It has a role to play when the question is one of handling dramatic budget cuts, and it will be addressed in the chapter on such actions.

Targeted increases have much the same effect. Where these are applied to library materials, the same procedures can be followed to determine the new allocations, with the difference that there will be more leeway, and it may be possible to differentiate between areas without penalizing those with lower levels of inflation and funding.

TABLE 5.1   Academic Library
Responses to Inflation

| | Past Year | | | | | | | Present Year | | | | | |
| | Original Allocation | | Actual Expenditure | | Rate of Inflation | To Meet Inflation | | Allowed Inflation | | Actual Dist. Maintained | | Modified Inflation | |
Area	$	%	$	%	%	$	%	$	%	$	%	$	%
Reference	158,500	15.85	159,210	15.53	14.00	180,690	16.51	166,425	15.85	163,065	15.53	173,350	16.51
General	83,000	8.30	82,840	8.08	7.00	88,810	8.11	87,150	8.30	84,845	8.08	85,190	8.11
Fine Arts	52,500	5.25	57,230	5.58	8.00	56,700	5.18	55,125	5.25	58,620	5.58	54,400	5.11
Humanities	74,300	7.43	74,880	7.30	7.00	79,500	7.26	78,015	7.43	76,700	7.30	76,270	7.26
Science	325,100	32.51	339,290	33.10	10.00	357,610	32.67	341,355	32.51	347,520	33.10	343,080	32.67
Social Science	153,600	15.36	152,960	14.92	9.00	167,420	15.30	161,280	15.36	156,670	14.92	160,620	15.30
Technology	103,000	10.30	108,620	10.60	8.00	111,240	10.16	108,150	10.30	111,260	10.60	106,720	10.16
Subtotal	950,000	95.00	975,030	95.11		1,041,970	95.20	997,500	95.00	998,680	95.11	999,630	95.20
Binding	50,000	5.00	50,100	4.89	5.00	52,500	4.80	52,500	5.00	51,320	4.89	50,370	4.80
Total	1,000,000	100.00	1,025,130	100.00		1,094,470	100.00	1,050,000	100.00	1,050,000	100.00	1,050,000	100.00

Notes:

The institution allows a 5 percent increase to meet inflation.

The areas as shown include all formats and various subjects. There will, of course, be internal variations, and these would be of concern when making the final budget decisions. Here the concern is with gross distributions only.

Handling an Overall Budget Cut

When an overall budget cut is required, the library has to determine its own priorities before any adjustments to library materials allocations can be made. The library must be aware of the effects of differential inflation throughout the budget. It may be possible, in some areas, to offset the effects of inflation by reducing the range or number of purchases, e.g., by reducing the numbers of telephones, or cutting back on supplies, or converting from all-inclusive maintenance agreements to service as needed. All such decisions carry with them hidden costs. Reinstalling telephones incurs added costs at the time of reinstallation. Supplies are an integral part of all library operations, and care needs to be taken not to cut back on essential items. Individual maintenance calls are usually more expensive than calls made under a general agreement. Most libraries already have had to look carefully at all such costs and have little fat left. Besides, all such general operating expenditures seldom amount to more than 10 percent of the total budget. Since the budget cut affects all expenditures, there may be little to transfer.

Such decisions may reduce shrinkage of the library materials budget, but, because the amounts likely to be saved are small, the cuts will still be sizable. They may total, say, 25 percent instead of 26 percent, a decrease that may not seem worth the effort required to attain it.

The same options are open as before. Possible scenarios responding to a 10 percent budget cut are set out in tables 8.3 and 8.4 (see pp. 75–77). An across-the-board cut will affect all areas. Here the caution must be that a standard cut will have a much more serious effect on small allocations, possibly reducing them to impotence. The need is to balance budget reductions against price increases to maintain an equitable distribution by subject or program. In order to do this, an allowance must be made for inflation in much the same manner as for too small an inflation allowance. In other words, all reduced allocations should be measured against the amounts needed to maintain the original programs; the goal should be to determine whether it is possible to maintain even a minimal program. In some instances it will be necessary to combine similar programs, leaving the internal distribution to those responsible for selection.

In public libraries the frequent effect is to close down one or more branches or to suspend some programs. In many ways, while still far from ideal, this option is better than attempting to maintain all services at far lower levels. Simply allowing collections to deteriorate may deter voters from attempting to improve the library's position and does not provide even minimal levels of service.

Approval Plans

Where approval plans or other gathering plans are being used, these will have to be reexamined and reduced in scope or eliminated entirely. If the plans are eliminated, some funds need to be redistributed to allow for individual selection. Most dealers supply information about the costs of various subjects, and it may be possible to eliminate subjects with a lower profile in order to maintain those with greater user need. Alternatively, it may be desirable to institute a price limit on books to be supplied automatically. All such decisions should be discussed, if time allows, with the dealers concerned, both to arrive at the best decisions and to alert the dealers to possible reductions in business. Whatever the decisions made, the result will be more direct ordering and more staff time used in selection. Where other modes are implemented, such as selection from *Choice,* new guidelines will have to be issued to selectors. These actions are necessary in order to prevent the library from running out of money early in the year.

The Mix of Materials

The mix of materials in each allocation will also affect what can be done. An area that is heavily serial dependent will have problems different from one where most purchases are of books. In such an area as chemistry, serials will probably account for 75 to 80 percent of the fund expenditures and may, moreover, account for as much as 10 percent of the total budget. Any substantial reduction must include the cancellation of serials, if any money at all is to be left over for other purchases and other subjects are not to be penalized. In areas such as literature, most purchases are of books, and the unit prices are also lower. Here it is possible to arrive at a compromise whereby marginal subscriptions are cancelled to enable the library to keep buying books. Neither compromise is likely to engender much enthusiasm, but the stark reality of not being able to buy either books *or* serials is likely to encourage cooperation in carrying out the cancellations. In this kind of situation, it is necessary to involve the user community and to consider levels of institutional commitment. Cutting back severely in a prime area of research is unlikely to win administrative support.

Handling Targeted Decreases

Targeted decreases simply offer a variation on an overall decrease and reduce the burden of choice for the library by taking over some basic decisions. Such external actions do not always take into account the ways in which the various parts of the library budget interact. If the library materials budget is exempted, the result can leave the library unable to process effectively all the materials received. For librarians, who are traditionally inclined to maintain collections, this can be traumatic as backlogs increase and operations become more inefficient.[7]

It is often very difficult to persuade nonlibrarians of such side effects, and the very separateness of the library materials budget has helped foster a sense that collection building is isolated from all other budget expenditures. This situation changes somewhat when program budgets are used. In public libraries, programs tend to be equivalent to library departments—e.g., Reference, Adult Services, Young Adults, Children's Services—and it is relatively straightforward to allocate all appropriate library expenditures in each program. Even so, larger public libraries have business collections or career centers, which have to be distinguished. In academic libraries, some areas of collecting are relatively easy to assign—e.g., Reference or Branch collections—but the remainder refer to user communities outside the library and share internal costs, such as selection and processing. Special libraries can assign costs by research project or by area of practice.

If the institution is using targeted decreases to prune, change, or eliminate programs, the library can use this information in deciding where to cut expenditures. Unfortunately, the information seldom is available in advance, and the library will have to make ex post facto adjustments. Use statistics and other service measures can help in determining priorities. It is not sensible (or sensitive) to cut back in popular areas. The best decisions can be made only with extensive information. Often the initial budget response can only be in broad terms. The actual work of determining final allocations will have to be undertaken as the new budget is set up, when wider information is likely to be available.

Transfer of Funds

In all settings, the degree to which the library is able to redirect funds internally will affect the initial response. If it is allowed to transfer funds between categories, it will be possible to take advantage of savings possibilities as they present themselves. Records of such savings from previous years will provide some guidance, but these will be affected by general budget decisions such as increases or decreases. The actual work of incorporating any savings into the new allocations will come after the beginning of the new budget year. It is not wise to reallocate "found money" as soon as it is identified. Some should be held in a reserve fund, both in case savings do not meet expectations and in case special circumstances arise during the year.

Resource Alternatives

When faced with budget cuts, libraries must pay serious attention to resource alternatives. Fred Lynden, speaking at the 1992 Charleston Conference, said he believed that all libraries should now budget in terms of resources rather than simply library materials. "Resource budgets" cover and include access costs and other alternatives to ownership. These may be as various as consortium fees or one access card to another library; as expensive as networked access to a databank or as cheap as a dedicated telephone to a service agency. On a more venturesome level, a fund may be established, from savings generated by serial cancellations, to pay for articles on demand.[8] In the longer run, such services will have to be supported by fees.[9] In the shorter run, they can be used to determine patterns of use and priorities.

Elimination of Programs

Another approach is to eliminate one kind of resource entirely. One public library, for example, decided not to buy any new videotapes (it had been spending roughly the amount of the budget cut on tapes) and to rely on gifts or use fees to add any new tapes. This kind of action is seldom available to an academic or special library, though an equivalent decision might be not to collect maps on a regular basis, or to rent or borrow rather than buy motion pictures. Sometimes, if an academic program is eliminated, subscriptions can be cancelled and certain kinds of books purchased only at a minimal level. As frequently noted, however, most areas within any collection are used by several constituencies.[10] Special libraries may be able to examine the alternative of on-line access and determine which subscriptions to print versions can be cancelled. Because their user groups and their needs are more closely defined, their collection needs are similarly well defined.[11]

Rethinking the Collection-Development Program

A very large budget reduction will force reconsideration of the entire collection-development program. Everything has to be considered *ab initio.* Here the traditional reluctance to cancel subscriptions (soundly based on the enormous difficulty of restarting them and filling in gaps) has often caused serious distortions within the collection. It is not possible to absorb a major cut without cancelling major subscriptions unless the library is willing to forgo planned book purchases. Even though many academics in the "hard" sciences claim that they do not use books, examination usually reveals their somewhat skewed vision of the latter category. Proceedings and reference works are not seen as books. What they mean is that they do not use what they think of as textbooks. This point of view also overlooks the needs of students or new faculty members who are becoming familiar with the basics of their disciplines. Moreover, perusal of any issue of *Choice,* for example, will reveal a substantial number of books suited to college libraries. It is, therefore, virtually impossible to eliminate the purchase of books in almost any discipline.

Public libraries have not generally invested heavily in the purchase and retention of serials. They do, on the other hand, purchase reference serials, abstracts, and indexes, all of which are basic to their mission. Major budget reductions will have a major effect on book-buying programs. Here the decision has to be whether to reduce across the board rather than penalize any specific area. The amount of the cut will be influenced by the unit prices of materials within each area. Paperbacks may be substituted for hardbacks, particularly in Young Adult collections, where use is heavy and fashions change rapidly. The higher cost of nonfiction may force larger cuts in this area than in popular fiction. Gathering plans may be suspended in favor of more selective purchasing, though it is possible that the added costs of selection and processing will outweigh any savings. Whatever method is chosen, new-book displays will be leaner. Where the practice is permitted by law, libraries may choose to purchase more copies for rental lending, thus trying to meet demand while still recouping some of the cost.

Use Patterns

All these strategies must be supported by extensive knowledge of use patterns. Without such data it is not possible to maintain an equitable response to user needs. It is even defensible to increase buying in heavy use areas or to pay more attention to repair and replacement, and to reduce expenditure in low-use areas more than might have been the case if cuts had been made across the board. These decisions can be justified by reference to use statistics, but care must be taken not to destroy the core collection by failure to replace out-of-date materials. It is better to withdraw such books as being misleading than to keep them simply because "they are all we have." This is one reason why public libraries and smaller colleges should make every effort to keep up reference collections. Another is that reference collections provide users with guidance to other materials which can be borrowed from or loaned by another library.

Cooperation and Coordination

In settings of budgetary pressure, cooperation and coordination become very important. Cooperative collection development is easiest for small groups of libraries. The work involved in coordinating serial cancellations, for example, can be very extensive and time consuming and is easier when libraries are close together and have compatible collections. Nevertheless, resource sharing cannot extend far down into the core collection. Each library must maintain what is needed locally. Sharing of collecting responsibilities does, on the other hand, preserve a wider range of materials than would be possible if every library acted individually.

Special Collections

It is difficult to maintain highly specialized collections unless special funds are available for the purpose. No library can afford to assign major funds from a tight budget to a small collecting area, but an effort must be made to continue at least basic additions, or the value of the existing collection will diminish rapidly. Only too often, smaller libraries fail to recognize that all libraries have unique or uncommon materials, thinking rather that special collections are the preserve of large research libraries. Of course most core collections are rather similar since they serve similar constituencies.

Even the largest libraries collect the same materials from gathering plans. It is the other purchases that add character to the collection, and these should be the object of cooperative endeavors. In this way all collections can be strengthened, even in hard times, without weakening the core. Public libraries with branch systems might also want to pay more attention to circulating loan collections, saving money by not purchasing multiple copies even while getting more use out of existing collections.

Planning Implications

Financial planning for these alternatives takes a great deal of care. There must be clear justification as a defense against those who see their own expectations deferred. One budget action might, for example, be the establishment of a postal fund to cover deliveries of materials borrowed through a cooperative, or funds to cover the photocopying of articles from cancelled journals. All such adaptations must be planned as proper extensions of collection development rather than simply being allowed to happen. Coping with change is always traumatic, and the immediate needs tend to overshadow longer-term considerations. Thinking through the consequences of each action will help to minimize later problems and ensure that the library continues to provide the best possible service consonant with the available budget.

Notes   1. Reference to any compilation of publishing data will show that library materials price inflation is higher than the general rate of inflation and has pertained over the last thirty years, even though there are variations annually.

2. *Higher Education Prices and Price Indexes, Update* (Washington: D.C.: Research Associates of Washington, September, 1991–).

3. If salary increases are negotiated separately, which means that the library does not have the discretion to make any changes, the result may be a pseudo–budget increase, even if other elements have been reduced. This phenomenon often turns up in surveys and other reports on library budgets. Even though it may appear that the library is receiving increased budgetary support, its purchasing power is being eroded. And increased salaries do not buy any more staff time.

4. Jerry D. Campbell, "Academic Library Budgets: Changing the Sixty/Forty Split," *Library Administration & Management* 3 (1989): 77–79.

5. Richard Abel argued strongly for the primacy of books in a paper delivered at the 1991 Charleston Conference. This paper, with others, is in the process of being published by JAI Press.

6. Richard de Gennaro, in discussing Harvard's need for storage, made the point that new construction on a central site would be expensive and might be impossible. On the other hand, remote storage, though costly, as new construction would more likely be able to satisfy the environmental needs of library materials, thus reducing conservation and preservation costs.

7. Interestingly, this effect also accompanied the rapid increases in library budgets in the 1960s. In one instance the author had to ask for a special budget transfer from library materials to personnel to have even the minimal staff increases needed to handle a greatly increased library materials budget.

8. An indication of possible savings gained by a switch from purchasing to borrowing can be seen from projections prepared by the Columbia University Library. *See Library Journal* 119,11 (June 15, 1994):44, which refers to Anthony J. Ferguson, Kathleen Kahoe, and Barbara A. List's *Columbia University Library Study* (Columbia University Libraries, 1993).

9. Recommended by David Taylor in "Serials Management: Issues and Recommendations," in *Issues in Library Management: A Reader for the Professional Librarian* (White Plains, N.Y.: Knowledge Industry Publications, 1989), pp.82–96.

10. Ongoing work by Chuck Hamaker of Louisiana State University confirms this point. He presented some preliminary conclusions at the 1992 Charleston Conference.

11. A paper prepared by a student at Simmons College Graduate School of Library and Information Science (1992) demonstrated clearly that a law firm could save money over the long haul by substituting on-line access for paper copies when the former included full text access. There has, however, been considerable discussion of the comparative value of LEXIS and WESTLAW because of the difference between their sources of data. Careful attention has to be paid to the total product, not simply to the bottom line.

Chapter 6

Serials and Databases: Access and Ownership

Although there are references throughout this book to serials and databases, their importance to budgetary concerns justifies their also being given separate consideration. For many years librarians have been dismayed by the soaring costs of serials.[1] Whatever the reasons behind this rapid increase in prices (causes cited have included the enormous increase in scholarly publishing, the labor-intensive nature of publishing, price gouging in a closed market, monopolistic publishers, unwillingness to face up to the problem, even comprehensive collecting policies), these rising costs clashed with diminishing budgets, to the degree that a true crisis emerged in the 1990s.

The advent of electronic publishing, together with the proliferation of databases and similar finding tools, has added yet another element of uncertainty. In addition, the new technologies have raised expectations on the part of library users. Libraries face a compound problem. They cannot afford to purchase and own all the library materials their users can identify and want to use. Those users expect to have ready access to ever-expanding resources. Bridging the gap between financial capacity and user expectation requires new ingenuity in library materials budgeting.

Serials and Databases in Collection Management

The role of serials and databases varies with the kind of library and with the subject matter. Public libraries, other than the central libraries in large systems, seldom invest a large proportion of their budget in serials. At the other extreme, many specialized libraries—law, medicine, and corporate research libraries, for example—may allocate as much as 80 percent of their budgets to serials. For the average general academic library, the old rule of thumb was that approximately 60 percent of the materials budget should be spent on serials and binding.

Within each institution there are variations. Typically, science and engineering libraries have spent 75 to 80 percent of their budget on serials, while the proportion in the humanities ran as low as 20 to 25 percent. The budgetary tables used in this book give examples of these distributions. However, as prices went up and budgets stagnated, these percentages edged upwards. Today, it is not uncommon for an academic library to invest 70 percent of its total library materials budget in serials. This upward shift has meant reductions in all other kinds of purchases. As if this were not enough, the cost of adding electronic resources must come from this shrinking residue. Many years ago the author pointed out that the inexorable result of soaring prices was that, within a relatively short period, subscriptions would absorb the entire budget.[2] In a few instances this actually happened, particularly when libraries suffered major budget cuts.

In a frank and somewhat disillusioned statement, Del Brinkman, vice chancellor for academic affairs at the University of Kansas, concluded:

> I can predict that American universities will be increasingly unable—and unwilling—to meet publishers' demands. More lacunae in individual collections are simply inevitable, and at some point in the future book acquisitions can no longer be sacrificed to continue the acquisition of serials.

He continued, speaking of access:

> Paradoxically, the funding for the instruments that allow one library to access another's holdings must further siphon monies that would otherwise go to the acquisition of materials.[3]

This statement neatly encapsulates the library's dilemma.

Serial Cancellation

To forestall such occurrences, most libraries review serial holdings regularly and cancel substantial numbers of subscriptions.[4] Even though some new titles are added, sometimes on a sort of one-in-one-out rule, this practice has, not unnaturally, caused much grief to scholars and researchers. No viable alternative has yet emerged. If libraries are to meet, at least to some degree, the reasonable expectations of most users, they cannot eliminate all books and other nonserial materials.

Cancellation projects require careful handling and the involvement of users.[5] The background concern must be whether some scholarly areas are being unduly penalized. Unless there is some consultation and cooperation, it is very possible that unique materials will be eliminated from whole regions. A survey of budget containment measures[6] revealed cancellation figures that suggest this effect may already be taking place.[7]

No one would claim any more that it is possible for any one library to meet all the needs of all its users. The price increase differential between disciplines has made the cost of maintaining serials in high-price, high-volume disciplines (typically science, medicine, and technology) so extreme that all other disciplinary areas are likely to suffer as a result, unless these costs can be curbed. The problem is that vital core journals tend to be very expensive and can be eliminated only in an emergency. Until such time as the mechanisms and costs for on-line access are fully developed, libraries must take great care not to cancel essential, heavily used journals.

Expenditure Proportions

Inspection of any serial subscription list broken down by subject reveals the range of the problem (such breakdowns can be provided by most agents). The first point is that a very high proportion of the total cost is generated in a very few areas, with a much larger number of areas generating relatively smaller shares. The second point is that within almost all subjects a few major subscriptions make up the greater part of that expenditure. Unless these prices can be held down, or the periodicals in question cancelled, major cuts will affect the other disciplines more heavily.

For this reason, it is inequitable to enforce across-the-board cuts. Chemistry, for example, may cost upwards of $100,000 a year,[8] with individual subscriptions costing over $600 a year and some key serials as much as $5,000 to $10,000. Comparative literature, on the other hand, may have relatively few subscriptions; they will total perhaps $2,500 a year at an average cost of about $50, with one subscription costing over $200. A 5 percent cut would take $5,000—six or seven subscriptions—from chemistry, but leave the bulk of the collection intact. A similar cut in comparative literature would take $300, or six subscriptions, and might wipe out an entire element in the program. In some instances, one or two expensive subscriptions may take the lion's share of a small allocation. To retain these in the face of budget cuts could mean the cancellation of virtually all others. As the cuts being made in library budgets become even more severe, this effect will be increased, until it is impossible to avoid the cancellation of core journals.

A somewhat more equitable approach is to maintain the budgetary proportions assigned before the cuts had to be made. This will, it is true, force deeper cuts in those high-cost areas with high inflation rates, but it will enable the library to maintain more than token collections in other areas. Where the users can be engaged more deeply in the process (not always possible in an emergency), it should be possible to encourage the cancellation of lesser-used high-cost journals even to the extent of making possible the addition of newer journals more in line with current research.[9] Neither of these approaches is flawless, and some changes may be possible as on-line access becomes more readily available.

The underlying problem is that new and important serials appear all the time, though at a lower rate than in earlier eras. While most cancellation projects have been budget driven, some have included a kind of carrot with the stick, using part of the money saved by cancellations to add new subscriptions.[10] Unless this is done, any library collection will lose value, which is a very different matter from costing less. The maintenance of any collection includes improvement every bit as much as looking after what is already owned.[11]

Collection Management and Access

Collection management includes making sure that what is owned is properly accessible and usable. The multiplication of on-line databases, added to the abstracts and indexes already available in print, poses a specific problem. Unless serials and books can be discovered by their potential users, for all practical purposes, they are nonexistent. The question is to match access tools with the actual collection, not only by being sure that materials are properly cataloged but by ensuring that users know that other materials appropriate to their needs are available, although not electronically indexed. There is also the question of the cost of providing bibliographical access via on-line catalogs and databases. These access sources cost money. There are direct and indirect costs. The latter were explored in a colloquy edited by Gail MacMillan[12] and include equipment, maintenance, staff costs, and service. These can be combined with the direct costs to provide a kind of investment matrix[13] whereby a library can determine substitutional benefits. By determining how to invest money for the greatest return, the library can decide how best to spend scarce dollars.

Beyond this, however, are the larger costs of collaborative access. Clifford Lynch[14] has suggested that the costs of establishing and maintaining a truly electronic library are much larger than most people think and can far exceed the cost of the present library. These costs are mostly for hardware and software, which, while important in the larger budget context, are outside the library materials budget proper but within the concept of a resource budget. Within the actual materials budget, one of the major costs is the retrieval of single articles, an activity which requires significant staff support expenditures in the interlibrary loan and document delivery categories. An even more troubling philosophical concern is what has been called the Wilson Library Index Syndrome. The indexes are largely based on what libraries purchase, and libraries tend to purchase what is indexed. This cyclical effect leaves a considerable area of publishing in limbo.

To a certain extent such publications as the *Alternative Press Index* provide a balance, but, by and large, indexes and abstracts tend to concentrate on serials already in the canon. On-line services concentrate even more on titles that are commonly held or in apparent high demand. In toto, indexes and abstracts, printed or on-line, provide information about many resources not likely to be in the average library and consequently leave the library with a sizable retrieval problem.

Use Patterns

Determining what serials to retain means looking at use patterns. Determining use is somewhat complicated, since most academic libraries do not circulate either single issues or bound volumes. Some surrogate measures are available.[15] These include reshelving statistics, which depend for their validity on the care with which users follow instructions. Some idea of use can be determined by examining volumes retrieved after being used for photocopying articles. In both cases, determining title counts requires the expenditure of more staff time than most libraries can afford. Public libraries, which generally circulate periodical issues, may be more able to determine user interest.

Much is made of citation studies, but there are some concerns as to whether these indicate actual use or merely the gathering of bibliographic support.[16] Many major journals are actually journals of record, i.e., they simply substantiate research already completed rather than actively supporting teaching and research. Some disciplines are relatively tight knit, with a small core of recognized journals. Others, particularly in the humanities, spread a wider net. Interdisciplinary studies, of course, draw on several disciplines and may inflate the usage in some areas. On the other hand, subject lists do not reveal the true extent of related serial needs, since no serial draws its readership from a single discipline.

These considerations require that libraries contemplating cancellations must consult groups other than those most evidently allied with the titles under consideration. Finally, all must remember that it is difficult to assign value to any use of library materials. All who use library materials have a valid need, and assigning primacy may deprive other users of their interest in keeping a lively library collection.

Electronic Publishing

The electronic journal is still too recent and untried to be assigned a place within the budget or the collection.[17] No clear cost pattern has yet emerged, but it seems likely that, in the future, use will be governed by contract, including membership payments as a variation. While it is difficult as yet to see exactly how copyright and royalties can readily be applied to these situations, it is already clear that extended use without payment may well be an infringement of the law. The present chaotic state of publishing on the Internet will be brought under some kind of control, and with that control clearer guides to use will emerge.

Other electronic services are becoming more common. These include bibliographic databases, which supplement and may replace existing indexes and abstracts, and full-text databanks. The latter are in their infancy, but the successful history of INFOTRAK (in hybrid form, with the text in microformat) suggests a ready acceptance among all types of library users. Once more the problem is that these databanks must be restricted in content to be commercially profitable, and users, unaware of this, may become equally unaware of what else exists. A more recent venture is The University Licensing Program (TULIP), an enterprise emerging from the Coalition for Networked Information, in which Elsevier Science Publishers has established an on-line, full-text database within a defined field and available to cooperating university libraries. A range of access levels is available. This venture may be the harbinger of future ways of distributing high-profile information. While such developments are testing the capabilities of on-line access, most libraries will have to continue grappling with how to pay for new services. As Michael Nelson noted, the high cost of databases may further erode the money available for resources actually needed on site.[18] It is hard, for example, to foresee a situation in which the learning needs of students, bound as they are by a term system and deadlines for papers, can be met from electronic resources alone. Nor is it likely that full text will soon be available for the multitudes of older published materials.

Beyond the efforts of individual libraries and publishers, there is springing up a new kind of document-delivery service. The most widely known is UnCover, first marketed by Colorado Academic Research Libraries (CARL), now an independent corporation. This kind of service draws on existing collections, international in scope, to provide articles on demand. Payments include royalties and may be quite steep. The object is to allow libraries to concentrate their own collections on basic needs, while ensuring access to a wide range of less-often-needed materials.

As these services expand and multiply, they can be expected to fill some of the gaps referred to by Del Brinkman, but, as he noted, they do not come without cost. Nor can they supply the whole range of articles likely to be discovered by library users. There are also various legal concerns as to how far access can be substituted for ownership, and they will need to be addressed. For instance, some court rulings suggest there are copyright concerns when document delivery is substituted for purchase within a multilibrary or multicampus system. Legal questions aside, in some cases of extensive need it is still cheaper to purchase than to transmit copies.

Some special libraries are moving speedily towards electronic conversion. This is most possible where the subject coverage is limited and the printed sources few in the first place. Law and medical libraries may find this kind of conversion easiest. Corporate libraries may be impeded until the manner of payment for electronic data is clarified. There are, however, many databases which are not available in the equivalent paper format—e.g., corporate reports—and which can be useful to public, academic, and special libraries.

All these services share two characteristics. First, they are quasi-serial in nature and will probably require continuing annual payments. Second, and different from all other published formats, they do not belong to the library; they are simply leased. A third factor, which has implications for the whole budget, is that they require hardware and software for use. The library may or may not be able to purchase either outright, but both will require annual service and maintenance. In addition, many accounting systems regard purchases of terminals as capital payments, and they may be subject to different purchasing controls. These observations do not speak to the systems' utility or importance, only to the fact that they form a new budget component with rather different financial rules than other library expenditures.

Budgetary Responses

Libraries will need to find ways to incorporate these services into their budgets. Because they incur continuing costs, they will have a permanent impact. To some extent, they may substitute for other ongoing costs, e.g., indexes and periodicals, but much of their cost must be found at the expense of other media. David Taylor[19] suggests that libraries will be unable to continue providing free access to database and document delivery services. In much the same way that free photocopying became impossible to sustain, so that libraries either had to levy charges themselves or utilize commercial services, he argues, unrestricted database access will necessarily come to an end. Fee for service has become a relatively common library fact. There are some legal and financial concerns. Copyright law decisions have narrowed the differences between for-profit and not-for-profit operations, and the Internal Revenue Service has been taking a closer look at such quasi-commercial services. It is quite probable that any fee-based service will be seen as conducted for profit and therefore taxable. Lest librarians should think that lack of profit can be a protection, it must be realized that any successful service must at least cover its own costs, including indirect overhead. If it is to be continued and expanded, it must also make the "profit" which enables the purchase of new machines and the like. It is quite possible that, fairly soon, these services will need to be separated from other library services, at least in a budgetary sense.[20]

Cooperation and Resource Sharing

A further result of extended electronic access is a far greater need for cooperation. Bibliographic access without the ability to obtain the cited materials is meaningless. While it is not possible here to explore the whole range of costs involved, certain kinds of costs need to be built into the new resource budget. Consortium memberships which support access, library cards, bibliographic utility costs,[21] and telecommunications costs need to be placed alongside library materials costs to create a true resource budget. Only in such a way can one truly assess the total cost of providing access to information, whether in local, owned materials or in resources located elsewhere. Any library that tries to decide on budget and program alternatives without such an assessment is groping in the dark.

Cooperation itself requires much more attention than the lip service it has generally been given. To be effective it must be planned. As the Aqueduct Action Agenda recommends in item 8, libraries need to share cancellation lists and their criteria for cancellation.[22] Even more, they must keep entries in union lists and union catalogs up to date. There have been few examples of extensive cooperation in collection development at the item level. Most cooperatives, such as the Research Libraries Group, operate at the level of assigning collecting responsibilities. On a small scale, the *Choice*-based selection process described by Rodney Erickson presents a positive model: three colleges agreed to cooperate to ensure that as wide a range as possible of *Choice* titles would be available within the group.[23] Larger-scale examples are reported by Sue Medina, who describes cooperation among the academic libraries of Alabama,[24] and by Eva Sartori, who recounts the cooperative development of serials within a region.[25] The mechanics of widespread cooperation can be complex and time consuming, but the benefit is the assurance that unique titles are not being cancelled and discarded.

Recognition of the need for closer coordination has led many computer-system vendors to make provision for their own networks, since sharing the same system makes many activities much simpler.[26] The same kind of extension of services is represented by CARL and UnCover, and there are indications that more vendors and agents are developing in the same ways. At a very basic level, there can be plans for last-copy retention (usually in public libraries and for fiction) and the transfer and consolidation of incomplete serial holdings. All these proposals have in common the recognition that, by cooperating, individual libraries can save money and still have access to a wider range of library materials.

While many of these activities may not appear to be strictly budget matters, the decisions inherent in cooperation affect local acquisition practices and therefore the library materials budget. Selective collection development, at least outside the inescapable core, will become the mark of a financially prudent library. Cooperation does not minimize the importance of making appropriate local decisions; it simply enables them to be made within a larger context. The result is likely to be a rather different budget distribution, but one which is based on careful decisions about the best way of spending the available money.

Notes

1. The highest level of concern has been expressed by academic librarians, but the facts are of importance to all libraries, if only because access to other libraries' holdings is becoming increasingly important. Among the many articles on the subject the following indicate the dimensions of the problem: Richard M. Dougherty, "Are Libraries Hostage to Rising Serials Costs?" *Bottom Line* 2,4 (1988): 25–27; Stuart L. Frazier, "Impact of Periodical Price Escalation on Small and Medium-sized Academic Libraries: A Survey," *Journal of Academic Librarianship* 18,3 (1992): 159–62; Robert L. Houbeck, Jr., "If Present Trends Continue: Responses to Journal Price Increases," *Journal of Academic Librarianship* 13 (1987): 214–20; Rebecca T. Lenzini, "Serials Prices: What's Happening and Why," *Collection Management* 12,1/2 (1990): 21–29; Paul McCarthy, "Serial Killers: Academic Libraries Respond to Soaring Costs," *Library Journal* 119,11 (June 15, 1994): 41–44; Myoung Chang Wilson, "The Price of Serials Is Everybody's Business," *Bottom Line* 3,4 (1989): 12–14.

2. Murray S. Martin, "Budgetary Strategies: Coping with a Changing Fiscal Environment," *Journal of Academic Librarianship* 2 (1977): 297–302.

3. Del Brinkman, "Some Thoughts on Maintaining University Libraries at State-Supported Institutions," *Scholarly Publishing Today* 1,3/4 (1992): 6–7.

4. Paul Metz, "Thirteen Steps to Avoiding Bad Luck in a Serials Cancellation Project," *Journal of Academic Librarianship* 18,2 (1992): 76–82.

5. *See,* for example, Karen Dalziel Tallman and J. Travis Leach, "Serials Review and the Three-Year Cancellation Project at the University of Arizona Library," *Serials Review* 15,3 (1989): 51–60. These concerns were also covered in three papers presented at the 1991 Charleston Conference by Donna Cohen of Rollins College, Amy Dykeman of Georgia Institute of Technology, and Connie Wu of Rutgers University, who all stressed the need for faculty involvement. These papers are expected to be published during 1995.

6. John A. Dunn, Jr., and Murray S. Martin, "Cost Containment in Libraries," *Bottom Line* 5,3 (Fall 1991): 23–24; and Murray S. Martin, "Cost Containment and Serial Cancellations," *Serials Review* 18,3 (1992): 64–65.

7. Initial research by the author in connection with the ACRL/MLA *International Bibliography* Scope and Coverage Project suggests that the coverage of Austra-

lian and New Zealand literary periodicals is unevenly distributed and that many titles are not held at all. This is a prime instance of major bibliographical coverage without corresponding library coverage. Discussion with other librarians suggests that the same may well be true in other "marginal" areas of study.

8. John O. Christensen, "Cost of Chemistry Journals to One Academic Library, 1980–1990," *Serials Review* 15,8 (1992): 19–33.

9. Frequent reference is made to the way in which Library Director Donald Koepp of Princeton worked with the faculty to resist price hikes by one publisher. His letter is referred to in the Aqueduct Action Agenda.

10. Thomas G. Kirk, "Periodicals Collections in College Libraries: Improving Relevancy, Access, Availability," *Journal of Academic Librarianship* 17,5 (1991): 298–301.

11. Richard M. Dougherty, "Exploding Myths: Clearing the Way toward a Redirected Campus Library," in *Proceedings: Conference on Acquisitions, Budgets and Collections,* edited by David C. Genaway (Canfield, Ohio: Genaway Associates, 1991), 11–22.

12. Gail MacMillan, "The Balance Point: Electronic Journals: Considerations for the Present and the Future," *Serials Review* 17,4 (1991): 77–86.

13. Murray S. Martin, "The Invasion of the Library Materials Budget by Technology. Serials and Databases: Buying More with Less?" *Serials Review* 18,3 (1992): 7–17.

14. Clifford A. Lynch, "Serials Management in the Age of Electronic Access," *Serials Review* 17,1 (1991): 7–12.

15. Maiken Naylor, "Assessing Current Periodical Usage at a Science and Engineering Library, a dBaseIII+ Application," *Serials Review* 16,4 (1990): 7–19.

16. This point has been made strongly by Richard Abel in numerous presentations. One such was given at the Charleston Conference in 1991 and is to be published by JAI Press, in 1995.

17. Michael K. Buckland, "Library Materials: Paper, Microforms, Databases," *College & Research Libraries* 49 (1988): 117–22; Paul Metz and Paul M. Gherman, "Serials Pricing and the Role of the Electronic Journal," *College & Research Libraries* 52,4 (1991): 315–27.

18. Michael L. Nelson, "High Database Prices and Their Impact on Information Access: Is There a Solution?" *Journal of Academic Librarianship* 13 (1987): 158–62; Ross W. Atkinson, "Old Forms, New Forms," *College & Research Libraries* 50 (1989): 507–20.

19. David C. Taylor, "Serials Management: Issues and Recommendations," in *Issues in Library Management: A Reader for the Professional Librarian* (White Plains, N.Y.: Knowledge Industry Publications, 1989), pp. 82–96.

20. *See,* for example, Yen Fong, "From Red to Black: Turning Around a Fee-based Service," *Fiscal Facts* 2,2 (1990): 8. The author describes the way in which the return on the Colorado Technical Reference Center was improved.

21. The Association of Research Libraries, for example, now includes data access costs under library materials.

22. Meeting at Chapel Hill, N.C., on February 7–9, 1992, a group of librarians laid out future actions that could be undertaken to support libraries in their collection management activities (*Scholarly Publishing Today* 1, 3/4 (1992): 7–8). These include actions addressed to the publishing community, to authors, and to librarians. The group will continue and monitor response.

23. Rodney Erickson, "*Choice* for Cooperative Collection Development," *Library Acquisitions* 16,1 (1992): 43–49.

24. Sue O. Medina, "The Evolution of Cooperative Collection Development in Alabama Academic Libraries," *College & Research Libraries* 53,1 (1992): 7–19.

25. Eva Martin Sartori, "Regional Collection Development of Serials," *Collection Management* 11,1/2 (1989): 69–76.

26. For an example of such changes the reader might look at the various publicity releases from Data Research Associates (DRA), which stress the ways in which that vendor supports cooperative activity. Notably, it provides Z39.50 servers and adherence to all requisite hardware and software standards.

Chapter 7

Setting Up the Library Materials Budget: Background Considerations

More has been written about fund allocation than about almost any other aspect of collection management. Good surveys of the literature have been prepared by Packer and Sellen.[1] However, these surveys emphasize what has been done in the past rather than the actuality of the present. Older methods of fund allocation were mostly concerned with the distribution of the money left after providing for serials, and this approach has provided little guidance in times of rapidly rising prices.

Vulnerability to external influences is a major factor in the handling of the library materials budget. Vendors and dealers have addressed the problem by providing forecasts, particularly for serials prices, but even "firm" prices can be changed in the course of the year, and there may well be extra charges for special supplements and the like. In many areas of scholarly publishing, libraries function as a virtually closed market, and some publishers have taken advantage of their position to increase prices far beyond the results of inflation. Some allocation formulas allow for price differentials, but most rely on internal indicators such as numbers of faculty, students, and courses. In any event, the actual dollar distribution is more a matter of what money is available than of an ideal.

If the librarian has been following the method of preparation outlined in this book, at least the broad lines of the library materials budget will already have been laid out. It should reflect what is desired, or, at the least, what seems possible within the general framework of the overall budget. Only when the final amount is known can true allocations be made.

Two principal factors may delay the final allocation: delay in the institutional budget process and determination of the amount of carried-over encumbrances. The first of these is outside the library's control. The state, town, or city may not have been able to arrive at a decision, or the trustees may have had to reconsider earlier budget estimates because of changes in enrollment. Until a final decision is reached, the library must operate under whatever rules are made concerning temporary funding. Usually, such rules allow operations to continue at roughly the level of the last year's funding.

But with decreases rather than increases the rule of the day, there may be other limitations, such as a set rate of expenditure per month or restriction to personnel-related expenditures.

A case can be made for exempting library materials from such limitations. Books tend to go out of print quickly and must be bought when available. Back purchases are always difficult and are in many cases impossible except through the antiquarian market. Serial subscriptions must be paid in advance, and many payments are due early in the fiscal year, enabling the vendor to place firm orders before the beginning of the calendar year. The author has found some instances in which no funds are released until the beginning of the academic year, which means a three-month purchasing gap, followed either by a lot of rush orders or by a filtering process which winnows out unobtainable orders. This kind of financial operation is not in the best interest of either the library or the parent institution. It delays an otherwise orderly process and telescopes ordering and payment into an unacceptably short period—essentially six months each year.

Unless all budget decisions are made in advance of the fiscal year, some delays can be expected. Unless there is a moratorium on all purchasing, the library should be prepared to undertake at least minimal purchases. Examples include books required for reserve reading and high-priority requests held over from the previous year. In particular, foreign publication orders may need to be set in motion because of the time required for delivery.

Care must be taken to ensure that such purchases do not distort the final distribution of funds. There needs to be a temporary budget with some limits on expenditure. With any luck, a final budget will be available before too long a time has elapsed, although the author has experienced both a year with no final budget and a year with three different, successive budgets. A good understanding with the budget officer can help settle how far the library should go. The purchase of very expensive items is unwise, but, even here, exceptions may have to be made when early purchase is accompanied by a substantial discount—a common practice with large microform sets and major reference works.

Finally, most large academic libraries have a variety of approval or blanket-order plans, and even smaller institutions have found it useful to adopt such plans at least in areas of concentration. Public libraries often have such plans for fiction and may also have standing orders for advance copies for use in branch selection. All libraries will have some standing orders for series or serials not obtainable through the usual serials vendors. These are most likely to be for reference materials and are thus essential for the functioning of the library. Materials being supplied through such arrangements will come automatically unless the standing-order or approval plan is cancelled. Since most orders would be reinstated, cancellation is a wasteful process: wasteful in terms of staff time, vendor frustration, and user service. This situation should be made clear to the parent institution or the governing board. It may be necessary to hold up payment until a final budget is passed, and vendors should be informed of this possibility.

Even though orders are placed and invoices received, payments may not be made by the institution until there are funds to cover them. For this reason, the keeping of careful records is mandatory. Libraries may be required to hold invoices—an easier situation to control than letting invoices pass out of the library's hands. The library's records should indicate not only an encumbrance of the order amount but that the funds are in essence spent. Such information will help prevent excessive ordering and make possible the maintainance of some kind of fund record.

Encumbrances

Unless the parent institution works under the accrual method of accounting, whereby payments are allocated to the year in which the order was placed, some amount of money will inevitably be encumbered at the beginning of the year. Snowball and Cohen describe the effects on fund accounting of an accrual system.[2] Nancy Stanley describes some of its positive effects.[3] To a certain degree, these principles can be applied to all situations by looking at annual variations, purchasing patterns, and long-term totals.

Most institutions, especially government organizations, work on a cash basis. They are budget driven. Each year's budget is regarded as a separate entity. No matter what is ordered, only that which is paid for counts towards that year's budget. Variations may be allowed. For instance, there may be a long or short period of grace during which invoices from the previous year may still be accepted. Other institutions put aside a set sum to meet late invoice payments; in this case the amount of time allowed for payments will be an important factor. Some adopt the more draconian practice of requiring that outstanding orders be cancelled. Luckily this practice is uncommon. If it is the institutional practice, the library must cancel such orders even if the intention is to reinstate them immediately.

The more common practice is to allow the buildup of encumbrances. This option recognizes the year-round nature of the acquisitions process and also that similar amounts will probably be carried over each year, so that in the long run everything balances out. The library that recognizes this fact is unlikely to overencumber heavily. More will be said about this practice in connection with monitoring the budget. Here the intention is to look at the effects of encumbrances on the allocation process.

Late delivery, delayed publication, invoices in overseas currencies, and problems with matching the invoice to what was actually delivered can all contribute to the buildup of encumbrances. It should be recognized that the library has two kinds of encumbrances. The first corresponds to the usual meaning of the term: orders placed but not received. The expected cost has been charged against the appropriate budget and fund but has not been balanced by a payment. The expectation is that at some time in the future both the material and an invoice will be received.

The second kind of encumbrance is represented by invoices on hand which could not be processed in time for inclusion in the budget year just ended. Whatever the reason, these invoices must now be paid unless there is a problem with the materials they represent. Here there is no cancellation option, and, what is more, it is undesirable to delay payment longer than absolutely necessary. What the library can do will depend on institutional practice. If there is a moratorium on payments of any kind, the library will have to continue holding the invoices. If not, even though the final budget may not have been prepared, the invoices should be processed for payment and the payments noted against the appropriate fund accounts.

Another reason for unpaid bills may be the internal processes of the institution. Invoices forwarded to the accounting department in time may simply not have been processed. This often happens when the amount to be paid must be converted from a foreign currency. Most institutions require that such invoices be handled earlier than those in dollar amounts, simply because of the extra time they require. In other instances, the omission may be accidental or the result of having too many invoices to process in a limited time. From a library perspective, these are the most difficult situations to handle, because the library has already included the amounts in its internal records. Only the process of reconciliation between the library and the institutional financial reports will reveal the amounts involved and their distribution.

The importance of such encumbrances to fund allocation is that they predetermine to some extent what allocations can be made. It is undesirable to set a fund at a figure which has already been wiped out by carried-over orders and invoices. It may be salutary to remind the staff or faculty member responsible for the fund that it is a bad practice either to order late in the year or to order materials too far in advance of publication. In other instances, unexpected events such as postal or shipping strikes or political problems may have delayed supply, without any fault on the part of the library. In such cases, it is desirable to make an allowance for the overrun even though it may cause some distortion in the "ideal" distribution.

Special Funds

In most cases, endowment and other special-fund income is not known immediately at the end of the fiscal year. Until the performance of the investments can be determined (and sometimes allocated among units), the actual expected income will not be known. For library purposes the income can be expected to be much the same as the previous year, but changing interest rates may change the return on investments. The effect on fund allocations will depend on the proportion of the total budget derived from endowments. Where these are extensive, increases or decreases in the rate of return can have substantial effects.

A second kind of special fund is that derived from grants or special budget allocations. In the sample academic budget being used to illustrate this book, a substantial amount comes from a National Endowment for the Humanities grant, whose annual income will probably continue at the same level. Other grants may be one time or spread over a period of years. These are good until spent, so that each year begins with the availability of what is left in the grant account.

Because these kinds of funds may be supplementary (i.e., they are not meant to replace regular funds), or integral (i.e., they are part of the total budget), their effects on allocation may differ. In the first instance, they should not be allowed to change the amount allocated to each fund. In the second, they are part of the total amount allocated. The second kind of special fund should, therefore, be taken into account when allocating among funds, while the former should not.

These factors suggest that, in any event, the library should not attempt to set up new allocations at the very beginning of the year. The delay should not be too great—in most instances only a month or so. This period of fact-finding and deliberation should also help the library to resolve held-over invoices and the like, so that the financial reports can reflect more accurately the true state of affairs.

Institutional Factors

Other kinds of factors that affect the budgeting process may be grouped under two headings: institution related, and library related. Institutional factors principally reflect the willingness of the institution or community to invest in the library. Here, Talbot[4] has shown that for academic libraries, the proportion of the total institutional budget devoted to libraries has not changed markedly over the years. Thus, spending depends less on library needs than on institutional attitudes. Similarly, public libraries often find that their budgets are controlled not by their needs but by the capacity of the funding authority to support many competing programs. The priority typically given to libraries seems to suggest that they are seen as overhead or desirable rather than central.

While librarians should not simply accept such an evaluation, an understanding of the ways in which their budgets are determined can help them to decide how best to use their funds. Demonstrating that spending decisions respond to user needs and improve the image of the institution or community is a primary marketing requirement.

Library Factors

Library-related factors begin with the existing situation, which carries with it some overwhelming imperatives. The most important of these, for academic libraries, is the division between long-term commitments (subscriptions and standing orders) and discretionary spending (books). The next most important factor is the differential between inflation rates in the various subject areas. Together these factors play the largest role in shaping the academic library budget, and the response to them may well be the single most important policy decision of the year. Although public libraries do not usually face the same degree of difficulty with serial subscriptions, they too find it difficult to maintain technical and scientific collections, especially if this must be done at the expense of popular reading.[5]

The second group of library factors relates to the programs of the library itself. Allocation formulas for academic libraries do not take into account the kinds of needs represented by reserve book and reference collections. Public libraries, too, have to consider how to maintain essential reference collections without weakening all other parts of the collection.

Reference collections—quite apart from abstracting and indexing services, whether in print, CD-ROM, or on-line—include many general materials which are not readily allocable to a subject or to a user group. Broad groupings, such as social sciences or humanities, can be used to guide expenditures, but many other general purchases are needed to respond to user requests: encyclopedias, dictionaries, books of quotations, and directories, for example. Reference departments often take on the task of "filling in the cracks" by selecting materials which are not clearly anyone else's responsibility. These collections are used by everybody and may legitimately be considered a general expense, but suballocations by broad groupings help in setting selecting policy.

There is also the question of supporting internal library activity. Much as institutions and governmental bodies allow individual departments to purchase basic directories and the like, libraries need to supply basic working tools for the staff in the various departments. In some cases these can also be made available to public users, but for the most part they will be in constant use by staff and thus unavailable to the general user. The library has, therefore, to decide how much it can spend for selection tools (duplicate copies of some periodicals, for instance), work tools (directories and manuals), and staff-development materials (library-science books and periodicals). Many of these purchases can benefit not only staff but user programs, amply justifying the existence of a general fund within the library materials budget for such purposes.

Gathering Plans

There is a growing possibility that the expansive gathering plans (blanket orders and approval plans) developed during the 1960s and 1970s may be cut back because of financial stress.[6] However, they are likely to remain a collection-development tool for some time to come. For one thing they simplify dealer relations and reduce the time that must be spent on selecting basic materials. For another, they help to minimize the danger that one will overlook needed materials which are not extensively advertised or reviewed.

Whatever the extent of such programs, you must allow for them in the budget. In earlier years it was time consuming to calculate their effects on subject distribution, but the emergence of analytical software has made it possible to determine what contribution they can make to the desired subject distribution. You can then see what direct allocations are needed to provide for other kinds of purchases to round out collecting plans.

Standing orders for series or sets also will play a substantial role in determining budget distribution. Music programs frequently have standing orders for long sets of scores, generally considered a top priority. Art catalogs may be the subject of a standing order or approval plan, since they often are very difficult to order on an individual basis. All such plans result in variable annual expenditures. In fact, because of this variability, standing orders offer the most trouble in predicting budgets. Nevertheless, because they are important, their effects must be taken into account, both in the overall budget and in subject allocations. Their cost may be high, but there still is a need to allow for other regular purchases if the collection is not to become moribund. It is important to consider all formats in the development of budget allocations.

Special Collections

Although the phrase *special collections* will suggest to most readers rare books and the like, nearly all libraries have one or more subject areas which receive special attention. There may be an important business collection or a career center in a public library, while an academic library may be particularly concerned with education or engineering. These kinds of emphases must be taken into account when allocating, since the goal is to maintain a responsive collection.

Another such concern may be participation in a cooperative collection program, in which the responsibility for collecting in a certain area is assigned to one library, which can, in turn, rely on other libraries to keep up with other subject areas. Cooperatives of this kind have fallen victim to decreasing budgets because it is difficult to justify the allocation of substantial sums for lesser-used materials. However, the library so situated does in fact have an important special collection which should not simply be allowed to wither.

The true special or rare books collection is a different matter. It poses a very real problem when funding is short. While extremely desirable within the national scene, such programs are, by their nature, luxuries, both by reason of cost and because of relatively low usage. The latter should be given careful consideration, because the individual uses may be of great scholarly or social value. From another perspective, they help define the nature of the library and the institution and may be a principal attraction for donations and endowments. Their role within the library has to be taken into account when dividing the budget. Strategies for dealing with these problems are discussed by Rebecca Martin.[7]

Like any other library unit, special collections should develop in accordance with a plan. Only too often, smaller academic libraries simply place expensive, fragile, or "rare" books in a vault or a locked room. A public library may have been donated a special collection it cannot afford to maintain or have a genealogy and local history collection without staff or budget support. In such a situation, it would be proper to review past practice and change it if possible. Properly developed, a special collection relates clearly to the goals and priorities of the library and the supporting institution and thus plays an active part in the library program. If this course has been followed, then it is appropriate to allocate funds for its sustenance.

The best strategy for special collections is to seek special funding from grants and gifts. These must be accompanied by an understanding with the funding authority that the extra funds are not to be seen as a way of reducing regular budget support. A second possible course is to provide for the use of savings or other special monies, or to recognize that the special collection may exercise some priority rights to reserved funds for especially important purchases. Care should be taken, however, not to accept gift collections (or those for which money is paid) unless they fall clearly within the library's priorities. Such gifts can distort the library's collections and impose added costs. Even well-intentioned gifts can become a kind of albatross unless properly handled.

Notes

1. Donna Packer, "Acquisitions Allocations: Equity, Politics, and Formulas," *Journal of Academic Librarianship* 14 (1988): 276–86; and Mary Sellen, "Book Budget Formula Allocations: A Review Essay," *Collection Management* 9,4 (1987): 13–24.

2. George J. Snowball and Martin S. Cohen, "Control of Book Fund Expenditures under an Accrual Accounting System," *Collection Management* 3 (1979): 5–20.

3. Nancy M. Stanley, "Accrual Accounting and Library Materials Acquisition," *Bottom Line* 7,2 (Fall 1993): 15–17.

4. Richard J. Talbot, "Financing the Academic Library," in *Priorities for Academic Libraries*, edited by Thomas J. Galvin and Beverly P. Lynch (San Francisco: Jossey-Bass, 1982), pp. 35–44.

5. "The Smaller Library," *Bottom Line* 7,2 (Fall 1993): 5.

6. Martin Warzala, "The Evolution of Approval Services," *Library Trends* 42,3 (1994): 514–23.

7. Rebecca R. Martin, "Special Collections: Strategies for Support in an Era of Limited Resources," *College & Research Libraries* 48,3 (1987): 241–46.

Chapter 8

Setting Up the Library Materials Budget: Allocation Procedures

The process of allocating funds is much more complicated than simply stating that the goal is to provide appropriate amounts for each fund. There has been much dispute over what factors are important and what statistical methods should be used to arrive at a distribution. The issue has been further complicated by the fact that most formulas deal only with the allocation of funds for monographs. One of the few exceptions has been the model proposed by Kohut, which attempts to include serials within a factor matrix.[1]

The use of automated systems allows for fairly sophisticated recovery of information, and several librarians have been developing this kind of approach. A good example is the style advocated by Brownson, drawing upon work done at Arizona State University.[2] He points to the political nature of the process and the problems in changing allocations and suggests ways in which libraries can escape from the rigidity of formulas without losing control.

The commonest factors used have been numbers of students, numbers of programs (or courses), numbers of faculty, and the like, often with elaborate weighting mechanisms. In addition, an inflation or price factor may be used. Few of these methodologies have been validated statistically because the meanings of most factors are subjective and therefore hard to measure.

Beginning with McGrath,[3] the factor of use became important. Usually this factor is based on circulation figures. While this approach can be a beneficial adjunct, it should not be the sole basis of fund distribution. Actual use levels in any area may vary from year to year, and the library's response should depend more on the existence of an academic program than on the numbers of people involved in it. Moreover, as Hamaker[4] and others have demonstrated, while any discipline provides a core of users, actual collection usage involves faculty and students from many other disciplines. This is particularly true of interdisciplinary programs, which cannot be directly related to any segment of the library classification system since they draw on materials used by several disciplines.

Moreover, use statistics require extremely sophisticated interpretation, and may not be at all helpful in very large libraries. There is also the imponderable issue of the value of any specific use. Should the library apply any weighting to faculty as against student use? And what is the value to the institution of each? Presumably, student use for learning and faculty use in research further institutional goals equally. Public libraries may be in a better position to use such information in developing their collections, but even for them, there is the question of what social goals are being pursued.[5]

Librarians should be aware that there is a considerable difference between use and user studies. The former are developed from statistical analyses rather than from the study of actual users. Use studies provide some link between collections and usage but do not directly link that usage to specific user groups. There have been very few user studies, and those that are available are mostly provided by publishers or learned societies.[6] As the author has suggested,[7] users roam throughout the library, making it difficult to determine any direct relationship between a scholarly group and a library classification sequence.

Even so, it is clearly in the best interest of libraries to have collections that are used, and proper weight should be given to evidence of use. This process may result in allocations that are not directly related to specific selectors or user groups, but it also helps the library to take care of those areas in the collection that are shared by many users, even though no specific department or program can be so associated. This finding will apply, of course, to reference and bibliographic collections and to general materials used by everyone. This observation makes a good case for a discretionary allocation fund and funds for general collecting.

New Measures

Other measuring techniques are emerging, made easier by the application of new software that can use information generated by the local automated system. An early example is the use of factor analysis to relate departmental needs to the supply of library information.[8] Later examples are the use of operational research methods as exemplified by Goyal,[9] or the classified course analysis developed by Palais,[10] and the development of a faculty research profile by Richardson.[11] These methods all deserve careful attention since it is now possible, using system software, to arrive at a much closer analysis of the collections than was possible when the first shelf-list count was developed.[12] In these ways more objective measures can be derived to balance the inevitably subjective responses from staff and users.

There is still no easy way to incorporate data on in-house collection usage or reference usage, though some sense of the latter can be derived from interlibrary loan requests resulting from database searches. By looking carefully at usage figures, it is also possible to determine whether any given trend is temporary or permanent. The difference is not always taken into account. Moreover, since most systems will record the level of user, it is also possible to see whether any given class predominates and whether the proportions change. These refinements can be applied to any of the earlier formulas with advantage.

Publication Factors

A factor that has received sporadic attention over the years is the actual amount of published material.[13] Werking's excellent review[14] covers the history of this factor, though, as has been pointed out, it still is difficult to determine either the size of book output by discipline or the cost involved. This challenge is made more complicated by the fact that the taxonomies used by higher education, the publishing world, and libraries all differ substantially.

Despite such difficulties, the likely size of the published literature, even if it is confined to U.S. publishing, can give some idea of the amount that should be set aside to meet the cost of acquiring current publishing. As an example, the amount of book publishing in education and agriculture, which can be very important programs in an institution, is much lower than the institutional involvement, suggesting that a smaller allocation would still meet the major needs of those groups. Similarly, many categories of publishing include materials that few libraries need to acquire—for instance, the devotional materials included under religion or the innumerable how-to and travel guides, which may be more important for a public library than an academic library. General figures should therefore be viewed with some skepticism.

For academic libraries, the kinds of annual surveys published in *Choice*[15] give a better picture of the relevant publishing. They cover the publications reviewed in *Choice* and so provide a useful insight into the relationship between selection and publishing. While they are most valuable to the smaller academic library, they can also be used by public libraries in building reference collections or special subject collections, say in business or art, and by special libraries for their own fields.

Their greatest importance here lies in their analyses of distribution. A couple of examples will best illustrate this value. The 1992 survey reported that education accounted for 92 titles (1.56 percent of the total) at an expenditure of $3,741, or only 1.43 percent of the total. By contrast, art and architecture generated 325 titles (5.50 percent of the total) at a cost of $18,811, or 7.17 percent of the total. Despite the fact that there were only three times as many art books, their total cost was nearly four times as great. Thus, buying a smaller number would still result in substantial expenditures.

The *Choice* annual survey table showing price increases over time also makes very clear both the distribution of inflation and its overall effect. One of the more surprising findings is that the rate of inflation is higher in the social and behavioral sciences than in science and technology. *Choice* does not regularly cover general fiction but concentrates on other genres of literary publishing, such as poetry and criticism; for fiction purchases, the totals would have to be adjusted. However, these figures still demonstrate the budgetary effects of price and distribution in publishing, which must have a substantial effect on how the library materials budget is distributed.

Other kinds of distributions could be arrived at by undertaking a similar analysis of reviews in *Library Journal,* and they would show similar results. In all such sources there also are reviews of other media, and the growing numbers of databases and other electronic media suggest that more attention will have to be paid to their distribution and cost in publishing analyses. For one thing they tend to have a higher unit cost than other media, and for another they are sometimes the sole source of certain kinds of information.

To the kinds of figures about American publishing found in *Publishers Weekly* and other sources should be added what information can be gained about the output of societies and institutions, many of which are highly relevant to research. Some of their publications are free and others can be obtained only on exchange; thus they cloud the allocation process but must not be ignored. Government publications are seldom included in publishing surveys but must be taken into account in making allocations. U.S. publications may be obtainable on deposit or for minimal cost, but those from overseas will have to be paid for. This is not as esoteric a suggestion as it may seem, since governments publish on topics that relate to all manner of disciplinary interests, and in some countries the government is the principal publisher. These and other variations will affect the direct application of publishing information to the budget, but, with care, such information can be used to guide the process of allocation.

Institutional Investment

A further factor that deserves more attention, particularly as costs soar in the sci-tech fields, is the degree of investment by the institution. This observation may appear to apply particularly to academic libraries, which are supposed to support academic programs, but it may also pertain to the effect on public libraries of population distribution, school budgets, and support of industry. Most colleges can provide data on the annual costs of each department or program, including support costs. The latter are important since they show how much added support such departments as engineering or chemistry need, say, for supplies and equipment. This kind of information often gives a much clearer statement of an institution's priorities than any written statement and can be used to demonstrate that similar library support is needed. In making such a case one should consider both the actual expenditures and the nature and extent of the teaching and research carried out by each program or department, since the library-related needs may vary greatly by discipline. The library can use other, more traditional factors to refine such a profile but should be careful to show that its allocations reflect institutional priorities.

The generally high cost of science and technology programs can be used to underline the need for parallel funding in the library budget; these fields are high-cost library areas.

The ways in which computer support costs are distributed varies greatly. They are usually regarded as a central cost, not as part of the cost of each program—though it is usually possible to determine who is using the most time. In earlier days computers were mostly used for number crunching, but this is no longer the case. The library should be careful to point out that the same reasoning applies to electronic information, which now may be as basic to the humanities and the social sciences as it has been for some time to hard science and technology. Because the library frequently is in the best position to further the transfer of electronic information, the institution should be educated by its library to understand that multiple subscriptions and uncontrolled access to databases may not be in the best interests of financial goals.

The point behind this seeming excursion into nonlibrary areas is to reinforce the idea that the library is an integral part of all institutional programs, so that all will suffer if the library is unable to provide appropriate information.

Library Application

The information gained from analyses described above needs to be transformed into a library-relevant format. Usually one needs some kind of classified approach, since this is the way the collections are organized. Classification systems often make it difficult to appraise interdisciplinary activities, but they also can turn up surprising results. As an example, when the author sought to classify courses taught at Tufts University, he identified a pervasive interest in the health sciences. Courses were found not only in biology, nutrition, and civil engineering, where they might have been expected, but in classics, history, and sociology. Thus, academic classifications often conceal divergent interests, which must be compensated for in any system of allocation. The librarian must always be aware of the kinds of research and teaching being pursued by individual scholars, since many of them will be working outside the supposed core of their disciplines. In the same way, public librarians need to be aware of special interests within their communities. The lesson is that it is too easy simply to rely on one system of assessment, and that it is best to use a double approach in developing a profile of interests.

Budget allocation for library materials must reflect the structure of the community. Standards, particularly those used by accrediting agencies, tend to use rather simple measures, such as the numbers of students, although this is changing as more emphasis is put on outcomes than on statistics. The need is to look at how well an institution is doing rather than at how much it is doing. For schools, as an example, increased emphasis is now being placed on how well students are learning to read, to write, and to perform mathematical processes. This demand motivates teachers and potential teachers to seek a supporting library that encourages individual creative activity rather than simply conforming to the syllabus, as education libraries have been wont to do.

In an academic setting, the relationship between the library and the institution is well described by Massman and Patterson:

> An academic library's holdings can be determined only by the quantity and range of materials being published *which are relevant to the academic programs* it is supporting, not by the traditional number-of-students criterion.[16] (emphasis added)

The key idea is relevancy. The numbers of programs supported are more relevant than the numbers of students. Institutional administrators and legislators, however, are inclined to count heads because so much else of the institution's expenditure is governed by the numbers of students. The 1986 *Standards for College Libraries* avoids this pitfall, though it still advocates a version of the Clapp-Jordan formula in calculating collection size. Such approaches are no longer relevant when budgets are falling and there are many changes in information-access mechanisms. The 1991 *Standards for University Libraries* eschews all reference to quantitative guidance and places more emphasis on access and preservation. Such statements recognize the importance of sensitivity to the goals and needs of the institution. As Dix pointed out many years ago,

> University library costs are related much less directly to numbers of students than they are to factors such as the number of fields offered, the nature of each field, the quality of the collections, and above all the research element.[17]

All librarians should also bear in mind the admonition of McGrath and his coauthors that "as with any statistical device [that device's] use is to assist in a management decision. The statistics themselves cannot make this decision."[18] The same kinds of arguments apply to other kinds of libraries, where the need is to remember not what the library wants to do but what the members of the community demonstrate they need, and use.

The attempt must be made to determine which factors are relevant to the library and what its needs are at a specific time. No planning is forever; both the needs and the capacity to meet those needs will change. Last year's distribution of funds may no longer be appropriate, but any changes should reflect actual developments and not simply be the result of caprice.

Basic Considerations

The first distinction that must be made in developing a library materials budget is between basic and augmentational needs.[19] Basic needs can be seen as those required to keep the collections alive and responsive to current need. In collection development terms, this basic consideration will relate mostly to current output in all formats. "Mostly," because there is also a need to replace worn-out standard materials, or those which must be kept updated in order to reflect user interests. The concern is maintenance of the collection.

Dealing with this concern is where most of the formulas come into play, since they deal with the cost of current buying. Once a distribution of current interests has been determined, it is possible to decide what investment is needed to keep up with those interests. Differential costs for various subject areas will have to be taken into consideration, since not doing so would skew any distribution in favor of high-cost areas. Also, the distribution of published titles will affect the amounts allocated. The use of a unit cost per subject has much to recommend it. Allocations can then be made in terms of units acquired rather than in terms of dollars spent. Unless there have been great inequities in the past, distribution by title among the various subjects is a good guide to the amount that should be expended to keep that distribution; hence the need to keep accurate tallies of the classified collection.

It is desirable to maintain some kind of ratio between expenditures on various formats. In earlier days—i.e., before the escalation of serial prices in the technical areas—a ratio of 40:60 between books and serials was regarded as optimal. Now that other kinds of media have to be taken into account this may no longer be true. Microform, database, and other electronic formats have to enter the equation, and it may be possible to maintain an adequate collection with less than 40 percent spent on books. Also, increases in purchasing articles on demand can reduce the need for the maintenance of costly but little-used serials. By examining usage patterns it may be possible to reduce some serial expenditures and plow the savings back into the more book-dependent disciplines. Books are less amenable to electronic access and may not always be available through interlibrary loan. Information from reserve book use and circulation records can be used to decide where there is continued use of books.

In a public library, it is likely there will be continued need for fiction, which is not the same as a demand for literature in academic libraries; the needs for nonfiction will reflect the current socioeconomic trends. It also has been pointed out that public libraries face great difficulties when reduced budgets almost force them to choose between keeping the reference collection up to date and supplying current popular fiction.[20] If a budget compromise cannot be reached, one or the other will be reduced to a very low level. In all cases, the aim is to maintain responsiveness to users, not to adhere to an artificial distribution.

Although it is fashionable to decry reliance on historic statistics, most libraries will find that use patterns do not change significantly over time. There may be shifts that reflect changing social attitudes, or that result from different emphases, but unless these new activities are additional to existing interests, their needs may be met more appropriately by altering the specific titles selected than by shifting budget allocations among subjects and media. There are exceptions. For example, in public libraries increased attention to the needs of physically challenged users may suggest that more money could be spent on large-print titles or on audiocassettes. In academic libraries, attention to the needs of underrepresented communities could lead to larger purchases of non-English titles or introductory texts.

The aim of maintenance is to keep the collection distribution much the same as it has been, but also to ensure that it includes newer materials in all areas. It is too easy to neglect an apparently dormant area, so that it does not receive this kind of upkeep.

Augmentation Needs

Augmentation is the process concerned with additions aimed at increasing scope or improving quality; at strengthening that which is; and with incrementational programs responding to changes in the institution or community. In an academic setting these will relate to back purchases intended to round out collections or to meet the needs of new programs or emphases. In a public library setting, they may reflect changes in the composition of the community, or social changes, such as new attitudes regarding health and nutrition. For example, a public library could determine that its collection of cookbooks fails to reflect current interests in cholesterol-free foods or that it emphasizes a specific kind of cooking and needs to cover new interests. An academic library might find that its collections unduly reflect a specific cultural bias or neglect whole cultural areas.

Social changes require that libraries examine their collections to see whether subjects have been underrepresented. For example, libraries in areas where there are large ethnic populations will wish to see whether the literatures of those cultures have been adequately collected. It may also be necessary to add to the collections materials to help users find their way through subjects that are most important to them.

Another kind of augmentational need, financial in nature, may be to provide some compensatory increase because of great price differentials. This has been particularly true in the science-technology-medicine area, where price increases have far exceeded those in other areas, but it is important to realize that price increases have affected all areas of publishing. Unless some compensatory action is undertaken, areas of great inflation could overwhelm all other areas. It may be possible to seek and receive added budgetary support to help maintain the balance, but, when money is short, it is more likely that a new balance will have to be struck. This may be done by reducing some kinds of expenditures, such as serials, by reducing book purchases in those areas, or by reducing expenditures in other areas. None of these alternatives is totally acceptable, though the first may be unavoidable.

The need is for a dialogue between the library and the various user groups to determine what is the best course. Here recourse may be had to the "just in time" theory of library purchasing. If the need for current information is for specific articles rather than for entire serials, it may be possible to reduce the total cost to the library by purchasing serial articles on demand. While the library may thus incur charges for royalties or article fees, the total outlay could well be less than the maintenance of serial subscriptions. In this case the augmentational cost is the cost of finding and purchasing individual articles. While this expenditure is not entirely a library materials cost (it includes personnel costs) it has to be regarded as part of the total resource cost to the library.

Allocations

With these considerations in mind it is possible to proceed to a budget allocation. The preferred mode is a matrix between programs and formats. In this way it is possible to see at a glance how much is allocated to each subject area or program and to each format. There will always be some expenditures that defy such an exact assignment—e.g., reference and general books and periodicals—but even the knowledge of these kinds of needed expenditures is essential for understanding how the library is meeting its goals.

TABLE 8.1   Library Materials Budget
Academic Library
5 Percent Budget Increase

Area	Books	Standing Orders	Serials	Data-bases	Media	Micro-forms	Totals	Percentage of Total
REFERENCE								
General	$ 2,800	$ 5,700	$15,000	$11,000	$ 1,050	$ 1,050	$ 36,600	3.49%
Fine Arts	2,000	2,200	9,500	3,100	1,050	—	17,850	1.70%
Humanities	3,650	6,000	15,750	9,200	—	—	34,600	3.30%
Science	5,000	7,900	21,000	11,000	—	—	44,900	4.28%
Social Science	2,825	2,900	5,500	7,500	—	—	18,725	1.78%
Technology	2,000	2,300	3,250	6,200	—	—	13,750	1.31%
Subtotal	18,275	27,000	70,000	48,000	2,100	1,050	166,425	15.85%
GENERAL								
Documents	8,200	—	3,500	—	—	2,100	13,800	1.31%
General	25,500	6,500	18,000	—	—	8,800	58,800	5.60%
Professional	2,000	1,200	2,100	—	—	—	5,300	0.50%
Replacements	9,250	—	—	—	—	—	9,250	0.88%
Subtotal	44,950	7,700	23,600	0	0	10,900	87,150	8.30%
FINE ARTS								
Art History	11,000	1,100	3,200	—	2,100	1,100	18,500	1.76%
Music	6,000	5,000	2,200	—	—	—	13,200	1.26%
Performing Arts	4,525	600	3,300	—	15,000	—	23,425	2.23%
Subtotal	21,525	6,700	8,700	0	17,100	1,100	55,125	5.25%
HUMANITIES								
Classics	5,000	1,100	3,200	—	—	—	9,300	0.89%
English	23,600	1,600	4,350	—	1,100	—	30,650	2.92%
Modern Languages	14,365	1,700	5,900	—	2,200	—	24,165	2.30%
Philosophy	8,000	400	5,500	—	—	—	13,900	1.32%
Subtotal	50,965	4,800	18,950	0	3,300	0	78,015	7.43%

The major controlling factor is the total amount of money available. The second most important is whether special restrictions affect any major amounts, such as endowments or one-time gifts. Together these factors determine whether it is possible to meet all requirements or whether some must be curtailed. Third, knowledge of what amounts were spent in each area during the previous year, together with an assessment of how well those expenditures met need, will determine whether there must be any radical departures from the earlier allocation pattern. Finally, knowledge of any new needs or programs can be used to decide whether there have to be corresponding decreases elsewhere or whether new needs will have to be met with new money: special grants or a budget increase.

Clearly, if the budget has decreased or simply not kept up with inflation, the situation will be very different from one where there is some increase. Although it may seem simplest to apportion any decrease across the board, this may not always be the best course, since it can penalize any program which has low funding and relatively low unit prices. A 5 percent decrease will be relatively more devastating to an allocation of $1,000 than to one of

TABLE 8.1   *(continued)*

Area	Books	Standing Orders	Serials	Data-bases	Media	Micro-forms	Totals	Percentage of Total
SCIENCE								
Biology	$ 3,100	$ 6,600	$ 86,000	$ —	$ 1,100	$ —	$ 96,800	9.22%
Chemistry	2,605	8,800	88,000	—	—	—	99,405	9.47%
Computer Science	2,350	1,100	7,500	—	—	—	10,950	1.04%
Mathematics	2,600	4,400	35,500	—	—	—	42,500	4.05%
Physics	2,500	2,200	87,000	—	—	—	91,700	8.73%
Subtotal	13,155	23,100	304,000	0	1,100	0	341,355	32.51%
SOCIAL SCIENCES								
Economics	9,000	750	11,700	—	—	—	21,450	2.04%
Education	5,900	1,100	10,600	—	2,700	1,600	21,900	2.09%
History	17,300	1,100	15,750	—	600	4,300	39,050	3.72%
Political Science	9,100	550	11,000	—	—	—	20,650	1.97%
Psychology	8,400	870	21,000	—	—	—	30,270	2.88%
Sociology	13,450	660	10,000	—	1,100	2,750	27,960	2.66%
Subtotal	63,150	5,030	80,050	0	4,400	8,650	161,280	15.36%
TECHNOLOGY (Engineering)								
General	1,800	550	11,700	—	1,100	—	15,150	1.44%
Chemical	1,900	550	14,000	—	—	—	16,450	1.57%
Civil	3,330	2,200	12,200	—	1,100	—	18,830	1.79%
Design	1,650	120	5,500	—	1,100	—	8,370	0.80%
Electrical	1,150	550	17,200	—	—	—	18,900	1.80%
Mechanical	3,900	550	26,000	—	—	—	30,450	2.90%
Subtotal	13,730	4,520	86,600	0	3,300	0	108,150	10.30%
BINDING	—	—	—	—	—	—	52,500	5.00%
GRAND TOTAL	225,750	78,850	591,900	48,000	31,300	21,700	1,050,000	100.00%
PERCENTAGE OF TOTAL	21.50%	7.51%	56.37%	4.57%	2.98%	2.07%	100.00%	

$150,000. For the smaller allocation, it may well represent two or more books; perhaps the only serial, costing $50, will need to be cancelled so as to sustain the purchase of needed books. In an allocation of $150,000, a 5 percent cut may mean the loss of two periodicals or perhaps twenty books, yet leave the bulk of the program intact. Some of these effects were explored in examining the results of stagnant budgets,[21] but much more work needs to be done to determine what kinds of expenditures are truly essential within each subject area.

For the purpose of discussion, simulated distributions are shown in tables 8.1 and 8.2. These distributions offer alternatives based on a small budget increase (5 percent), not enough to allow for the full effects of inflation but enough to enable the library to continue its programs.

By way of comparison, the same ideas have been applied to a 10 percent budget decrease. The results are shown in tables 8.3 and 8.4. These budgets show the different outcomes in various areas which give different priorities to standing orders and serials than to "books." The library, in both cases, has decided to continue its database program at the same level. Nevertheless, it

TABLE 8.2   Library Materials Budget
Public Library
5 Percent Budget Increase

Area	Books	Standing Orders	Serials	Data-bases	Media	Total	Percentage of Total
REFERENCE	$ 12,925	$18,000	$ 5,000	$14,400	$ 500	$ 50,825	19.36%
ADULT							
Nonfiction	43,800	0	0	0	3,500	47,300	18.02%
Business (1)	4,000	2,500	3,400	3,200	1,000	14,100	5.37%
Careers (2)	2,000	500	2,000	2,000	800	7,300	2.78%
Periodicals	0	0	55,000	0	0	55,000	20.95%
Audiovisuals	0	0	0	0	11,000	11,000	4.19%
Gen. Fiction	30,500	0	0	0	0	30,500	11.62%
Mystery	2,450	0	0	0	0	2,450	0.93%
Romance	2,225	0	0	0	0	2,225	0.85%
Paperbacks	2,400	0	0	0	0	2,400	0.91%
Rental (3)	[6,500]		0	0	0	[6,500]	
Large Print	3,500	0	0	0	0	3,500	1.33%
Subtotal	90,875	3,000	60,400	5,200	16,300	175,775	66.96%
YOUNG ADULT							
Nonfiction	3,250	0	600	0	0	3,850	1.47%
Fiction	6,275	0	0	0	0	6,275	2.39%
Audiovisuals	0	0	0	0	4,100	4,100	1.56%
Subtotal	9,525	0	600	0	4,100	14,225	5.42%
CHILDREN							
Reference	2,600	0	1,100	2,100	0	5,800	2.21%
Nonfiction	3,100	0	0	0	0	3,100	1.18%
Fiction	5,300	0	0	0	0	5,300	2.02%
Picture Books	6,275	0	0	0	0	6,275	2.39%
Audiovisuals	0	0	0	0	1,200	1,200	0.46%
Subtotal	17,275	0	1,100	2,100	1,200	21,675	8.26%
GRAND TOTAL	130,600	21,000	67,100	21,700	22,100	262,500	100.00%
PERCENTAGE OF TOTAL	49.75%	8.00%	25.56%	8.27%	8.42%	100.00%	

will be necessary to cancel some subscriptions and to reduce the number of books purchased. The decisions will vary by discipline or user group.

These budgets have been based on the concept of retaining the same percentage distribution among programs. As can be seen from a glance at these figures and a comparison with the earlier budgets, most programs will have to cut back in some formats, particularly serials. In partial compensation, database expenditure has been maintained, providing access for resource-sharing information.

Different decisions have been made in different areas. Some—e.g., music—have opted to retain standing orders; others—e.g., chemistry and the other sciences—have opted to retain serials, though here there has been a corresponding decrease in the allocation for books. Despite the apparent increase in total funds, the allocations do not meet the price increases that seem likely, and a number of serials will have to be cancelled.

TABLE 8.3   Library Materials Budget
Academic Library
10 Percent Budget Decrease

Area	Books	Standing Orders	Serials	Data-bases	Media	Micro-forms	Total	Percentage of Total
REFERENCE								
General	$ 2,900	$ 5,000	$12,000	$11,000	$ 500	$ 500	$ 31,900	3.54%
Fine Arts	1,800	1,700	7,000	3,100	500	—	14,100	1.57%
Humanities	3,800	5,000	13,000	9,000	—	—	30,800	3.42%
Science	4,000	7,000	15,600	10,000	—	—	36,600	4.07%
Social Science	2,700	2,500	4,000	7,500	—	—	16,700	1.86%
Technology	1,750	1,800	2,800	6,200	—	—	12,550	1.39%
Subtotal	16,950	23,000	54,400	46,800	1,000	500	142,650	15.85%
GENERAL								
Documents	7,500	—	2,700	—	—	2,000	12,200	1.36%
General	23,300	5,000	15,000	—	—	5,000	48,300	5.37%
Professional	1,600	900	1,700	—	—	—	4,200	0.47%
Replacements	10,000	—	—	—	—	—	10,000	1.11%
Subtotal	42,400	5,900	19,400	0	0	7,000	74,700	8.30%
FINE ARTS								
Art History	9,250	1,000	2,900	—	1,700	1,000	15,850	1.76%
Music	3,500	5,600	1,900	—	—	—	11,000	1.22%
Performing Arts	3,000	500	2,900	—	14,000	—	20,400	2.27%
Subtotal	15,750	7,100	7,700	0	15,700	1,000	47,250	5.25%
HUMANITIES								
Classics	4,800	500	2,700	—	—	—	8,000	0.89%
English	22,000	900	3,600	—	600	—	27,100	3.01%
Modern Languages	12,770	1,000	4,600	—	1,500	—	19,870	2.21%
Philosophy	7,000	300	4,600	—	—	—	11,900	1.32%
Subtotal	46,570	2,700	15,500	0	2,100	0	66,870	7.43%

(continued)

Another kind of distribution would try to allow for inflation by providing increases for the areas most affected. This approach reduces the purchasing power of all the other areas but still does not compensate for the full impact of price increases. In effect, it has weakened all the other programs. This dilemma faces all libraries during economic hard times. The author recommends the method which retains an equal percentage distribution, because it is the one which is most easily justifiable. Some compensation can be found by moving funds to provide access rather than ownership, but this option also requires that the library reconsider its whole budget.

Of course, there can be adjustments to the initial budget run. Once it is possible to estimate the effects of the new budget, all librarians should fine-tune their response. This may mean recasting the budget, but it is less traumatic than having to explain why the library is unable to meet user needs.

In more down-to-earth language, the budget allocation should aim to cope adequately with commitments and inflation, but it may not always be possible to do so. The simple maintenance of subscriptions within a fixed budget, or even one with a minimal increase, would reduce all other kinds

TABLE 8.3   *(continued)*

Area	Books	Standing Orders	Serials	Data-bases	Media	Micro-forms	Total	Percentage of Total
SCIENCE								
Biology	$ 5,000	$ 4,000	$ 72,000	$ —	$ —	$ —	$ 81,000	9.00%
Chemistry	4,300	3,000	80,000	—	—	—	87,300	9.70%
Computer Science	2,800	1,000	5,000	—	—	—	8,800	0.98%
Mathematics	2,990	3,000	30,000	—	—	—	35,990	4.00%
Physics	3,000	1,500	75,000	—	—	—	79,500	8.83%
Subtotal	18,090	12,500	262,000	0	0	0	292,590	32.51%
SOCIAL SCIENCES								
Economics	8,240	600	10,000	—	—	—	18,840	2.09%
Education	5,200	1,000	9,500	—	2,100	1,400	19,200	2.13%
History	16,400	1,000	13,500	—	—	2,000	32,900	3.66%
Political Science	8,000	400	9,000	—	—	—	17,400	1.93%
Psychology	7,800	600	18,000	—	—	—	26,400	2.93%
Sociology	13,500	500	8,500	—	1,000	—	23,500	2.61%
Subtotal	59,140	4,100	68,500	0	3,100	3,400	138,240	15.36%
TECHNOLOGY (Engineering)								
General	1,500	—	10,000	—	1,000	—	12,500	1.39%
Chemical	1,600	500	12,000	—	—	—	14,100	1.57%
Civil	3,000	1,500	10,000	—	1,000	—	15,500	1.72%
Design	1,600	—	4,700	—	1,000	—	7,300	0.81%
Electrical	1,000	500	14,000	—	—	—	15,500	1.72%
Mechanical	3,800	500	23,500	—	—	—	27,800	3.09%
Subtotal	12,500	3,000	74,200	0	3,000	0	92,700	10.30%
BINDING	—	—	—	—	—	—	45,000	5.00%
GRAND TOTAL	211,400	58,300	501,700	46,800	24,900	11,900	900,000	100.00%
PERCENTAGE OF TOTAL	23.49%	6.48%	55.74%	5.20%	2.77%	1.32%	100.00%	

of purchases, eventually to an unacceptable level. Moreover, it would inexorably change the distribution among programs or subject areas. Because inflation is unevenly distributed and publishers' charges vary among areas, the average of these variables cannot be used as a unique predictor. An average flattens the differences (the reason for not making across-the-board cuts) and eventually favors those areas with the highest inflation rates. In the long run, high-cost areas can only be maintained at the expense of areas where cost increases are not so high. These facts show the difficulty of keeping a library where it is. Unless it is possible to match inflation completely, there will inevitably be changes in library responsiveness.

The question that has to be asked of the administration is whether this kind of change is acceptable to the institution. As Baumol and Marcus pointed out some years ago, "society can, if it chooses, meet these rising costs."[22] The problem faced by most libraries arises from the conditional clause—a reminder that political motives, at least as much as economic ones, control the setting of budgets.

TABLE 8.4   Library Materials Budget
Public Library
10 Percent Budget Decrease

Area	Books	Standing Orders	Serials	Data-bases	Media	Total	Percentage of Total
REFERENCE	$ 10,050	$15,000	$ 4,000	$14,400	$ 200	$ 43,650	19.40%
ADULT							
Nonfiction	37,000	0	0	0	2,500	39,500	17.56%
Business	3,000	1,700	3,200	3,000	500	11,400	5.07%
Careers	1,700	500	2,000	2,000	700	6,900	3.07%
Periodicals	0	0	46,000	0	0	46,000	20.44%
Audiovisuals	0	0	0	0	10,000	10,000	4.44%
Gen. Fiction	27,650	0	0	0	0	27,650	12.29%
Mystery	2,200	0	0	0	0	2,200	0.98%
Romance	1,500	0	0	0	0	1,500	0.67%
Paperbacks	2,200	0	0	0	0	2,200	0.98%
Rental	[6,500]		0	0	0	[6,500]	
Large Print	3,400	0	0	0	0	3,400	1.51%
Subtotal	78,650	2,200	51,200	5,000	13,700	150,750	67.00%
YOUNG ADULT							
Nonfiction	2,600	0	500	0	0	3,100	1.38%
Fiction	5,550	0	0	0	0	5,550	2.47%
Audiovisuals	0	0	0	0	3,500	3,500	1.56%
Subtotal	8,150	0	500	0	3,500	12,150	5.40%
CHILDREN							
Reference	1,150	0	800	2,100	0	4,050	1.80%
Nonfiction	2,600	0	0	0	0	2,600	1.16%
Fiction	4,800	0	0	0	0	4,800	2.13%
Picture Books	6,000	0	0	0	0	6,000	2.67%
Audiovisuals	0	0	0	0	1,000	1,000	0.44%
Subtotal	14,550	0	800	2,100	1,000	18,450	8.20%
GRAND TOTAL	111,400	17,200	56,500	21,500	18,400	225,000	100.00%
PERCENTAGE OF TOTAL	49.51%	7.64%	25.11%	9.56%	8.18%	100.00%	

In a time when institutional budgets in general are not keeping pace with inflation, the library cannot expect to be spared. Very hard questions are likely to be asked about the need for the kinds of expenditures recommended, and suggestions made for reducing them. Useful discussion of the effects of serial price increases can be found in articles by Lenzini,[23] who discusses what has been happening to serial prices; Houbeck[24] and Dougherty,[25] who investigate the effects on academic libraries; and White,[26] who disputes the kinds of responses adopted by libraries. These articles may seem to present a negative view but are essential for the understanding of what is happening to library materials budgets.

These changes are external to libraries and therefore not under their control—a fact that often escapes administrators. Even so, libraries will need to seek other solutions, and cooperative collection development offers one way of coping with these changes. Libraries should be aware, however, that cooperation agreements mean a continuing commitment to specific purchases. Sartori[27] describes the ways in which regional cooperation can help libraries reduce individual expenditures. Moreover, even while consideration may be being given to cancellations, there is the need to decide what kinds of new subscriptions must be added, simply to keep the collection alive.[28]

The primary reason for any collection-development policy is to ensure that the library continues to be able to respond to need. Some adjustments can be made, based on the availability of on-line databases (including full-text databases), but heavy local use still seems to require access to the printed versions, particularly of books, unless the institution can guarantee sufficient points of access to machine records. Some of these issues were addressed at OCLC's Twelfth Annual Conference of Research Library Directors. Brian Hawkins urged libraries to plan for a national electronic library, saying "The library of the future will be less a place where information is kept than a portal though which students and faculty will access the vast information resources of the world." Robert Hayes stressed that the electronic future should not be seen as the solution of economic problems and that "the new media must be considered, not only in their own right but as essential adjuncts and supplements to the printed formats."[29]

On-line databases—owned, leased, or accessed—can substitute for serials or serial services and may lessen the impact of price increases on other kinds of purchases. But they carry with them their own budget impacts. These are discussed by Michael Nelson;[30] they should be studied by all librarians as they attempt to incorporate the new technologies.

It is essential to remember that the allocation of annual funds for library materials concerns the distribution of actual funds, not of an ideal amount. Ideals, goals, and comparisons are essential when formulating a budget request. When the chips are down and the budget has been set, only existing facts can be taken into account. Funds must be set aside to meet existing commitments, whether encumbrances or serial purchases, but those commitments must always be examined in terms of their long-term effects.

Because all institutions must undertake contingency planning, libraries cannot rely on guaranteed budgets. Sometimes added funds become available, but more often there will be assessments to provide for more pressing needs.

So far as is possible, guaranteed funds must be used to support essential programs. Not everything that is published needs to be bought. Even if it were possible, it would be undesirable, since much that is published is redundant, below the necessary quality levels, or irrelevant to the library's mission. But it must be stressed that current publications are most easily acquired within a short time after publication and also have their greatest use during the first one or two years. There is also the need to replace lost, stolen, or mutilated materials which are still in high demand, and to provide for binding and repair. These kinds of expenditures represent the maintenance of the collection at a usable level and therefore have first call on the budget.

The object of the process being discussed is to produce a budget distribution which provides for each area or program, but which is not so rigid that fortuitous circumstances or internal changes cannot be accommodated. Some reserve funds are essential to provide for such chance happenings.

The distribution should reflect the organization of the library. The individual accounts should be no more in number than are needed to meet this goal and should not be so small in size that the labor of maintaining the records exceeds the value of the fund.

In keeping with the general goal of program budgets, which is to improve control of program expenditures, accounts should be set up to support the exercise of professional judgment in purchasing one kind of material as against another, provided that there is some general supervision of such permanent commitments as subscriptions. Each account or fund should be assignable to one person, even if that person should control several accounts or work with others in deciding purchases. Such a course makes it easier to assign authority, responsibility, and control.

The final result should be a kind of matrix which assigns funds (and the responsibility for them) to individual selectors, and which summarizes them by category and financial source. It is recognized that this or any other method may not be available to or suitable for a specific library, but the proposal illustrates ways in which a library can recognize multiple responsibilities.

Notes

1. J. Kohut, "Allocating the Budget: An Economic Model," *College & Research Libraries* 35 (1974): 192–99.

2. Charles W. Brownson, "Modeling Library Materials Expenditure: Initial Experiments at Arizona State University," *Library Resources & Technical Services* 35 (1991): 87–103.

3. Willam E. McGrath, "A Programmatic Book Allocation Formula for Academic and Public Libraries, with a Test for Its Effectiveness," *Library Resources & Technical Services* 13 (1975): 356–69.

4. In a paper on the use of engineering collections, presented at the 1992 Charleston Conference on Acquisitions, Charles Hamaker pointed out that most of the use of these collections was by nonengineers. Also see Paul Metz, *The Landscape of Literature: Use of Subject Collections in a University Library* (Chicago: ALA, 1983), which generally supports this thesis.

5. John N. Berry III, "Redwood City Public Library," *Library Journal* 117,11 (1992): 32–35, and Nancy Pearl and Gregory Buthod, "Upgrading the 'McLibrary,'" *Library Journal* 117,17 (1992): 37–39, present two different ways of arriving at a definition of goals.

6. Advertisements for Elsevier in several library periodicals present one side of the issue. Another side is shown in the various considerations of scholarly publishing today, for example the landmark study *Scholarly Communication: The Report of the National Enquiry* (Baltimore: Johns Hopkins University Press, 1979), and the more recent changes addressed by John Budd in "Not What It Used to Be: Scholarly Communication Then and Now," in *Scholarly Communication in an Electronic Environment,* edited by R. S. Martin (Chicago: ACRL, 1993), pp. 1–19.

7. Murray S. Martin, "Captain James Cook: Postage Stamps and Collection Management," *Collection Management* 18,1/2 (1993): 11–20.

8. William E. McGrath, Ralph C. Huntsinger, and Gary R. Barker, "An Allocation Formula Derived from a Factor Analysis of Academic Departments," *College & Research Libraries* 30 (1969): 51–62.

9. S. K. Goyal, "Allocation of Library Funds to Different Departments of a University—an Operations Research Approach," *College & Research Libraries* 34 (1973): 219–22.

10. Elliot Palais, "Use of Course Analysis in Computing a Collection Development Policy Statement for a University Library," *Journal of Academic Librarianship* 13 (1987): 8–17.

11. Jeanne M. Richardson, "Faculty Research Profile Created for Use in a University Library," *Journal of Academic Librarianship* 16 (1990): 154–57.

12. A large number of academic libraries have been participating in a shelf-list count project for more than two decades. The object has been to determine how collections have been growing, without having to undertake the arduous activities associated with the application of the Research Libraries Group Conspectus.

13. William Randall, "The College Library Book Budget," *Library Quarterly* 1 (1931): 421–25, provides the first such reference.

14. Richard Werking, "Allocating the Academic Library's Book Budget: Historical Perspectives and Current Perspectives," *Journal of Academic Librarianship* 14 (1988): 140–44.

15. "College Book Price Information," usually in the March or April issue of *Choice*. The figures cited in the text come from the study for 1992, *Choice* 30,7 (1993): 1083–89.

16. Virgil F. Massman and Kelly Patterson, "A Minimum Budget for Current Acquisitions," *College & Research Libraries* 31 (1970): 83–88.

17. William S. Dix, "The Financing of College Libraries," *College & Research Libraries* 35 (1975): 252–57.

18. William E. McGrath, "A Programmatic Book Allocation For Academic and Public Libraries, with a Test for Its Effectiveness," *Library Resources & Technical Services* 13 (1975): 362.

19. Jasper C. Schad, "Allocating Book Funds: Control or Planning," *College & Research Libraries* 31 (1970): 155–59 is one of several articles on the topic. Useful definitions are provided in *Higher Education Prices and Price Indexes* (Washington, D.C.: Research Associates of Washington, 1990 update), pp. 28–30.

20. A recent example was provided by the librarian of the Warehouse Point (Conn.) Public Library, in remarks to the *Hartford Courant*, where he pointed out that the library reference collection was out of date and that he had opted to reduce expenditures on popular fiction in order to improve it.

21. Murray S. Martin, "The Implications for Acquisitions of Stagnant Budgets," *Acquisitions Librarian* 2 (1989), 105–17.

22. William J. Baumol and Matityahu Marcus, *The Economics of Academic Libraries* (Washington, D.C.: American Council on Education, 1973), pp. 56–57.

23. Rebecca T. Lenzini, "Serials Prices: What's Happening and Why," *Collection Management* 12,1/2 (1990): 21–29.

24. Robert L. Houbeck, Jr., "If Present Trends Continue: Responding to Journal Price Increases," *Journal of Academic Librarianship* 13 (1987): 214–22.

25. Richard M. Dougherty, "Are Libraries Hostage to Rising Serial Costs?" *Bottom Line* 2,4 (1988): 25–27.

26. Herbert S. White, "Getting into This Mess Wasn't Easy! It Took a Lot of Effort on Our Part," *Technical Services Quarterly* 8: 3–16.

27. Eva Martin Sartori, "Regional Collection Development of Serials," *Collection Management* 11,1/2 (1989): 69–76.

28. Richard Dougherty in an oral presentation, "Exploding the Myths: Clearing the Way to a Directed Campus Library," to the Acquisitions '91 Conference, Minneapolis, 1991.

29. Nancy Campbell, "Directors of Research Libraries Attend Annual Conference at OCLC," *OCLC Newsletter* 209 (May/June 1994): 4–6.

30. Michael L. Nelson, "High Database Prices and Their Impact on Information Access," *Journal of Academic Librarianship* 13 (1987): 158–62.

Chapter 9

Monitoring the Library Materials Budget

The three basic reasons for monitoring expenditure are

1. to determine whether the budget is being expended in accordance with the library plan;
2. to determine whether all encumbrances and payments are correctly recorded;
3. to determine whether the budget has been spent or whether there are any unspent funds.

These reasons apply to all sections of the library budget. All budget lines or categories are set with a purpose. In some cases, e.g., salaries and wages, the library need do little direct monitoring, but in others, where there is more discretionary spending, it is necessary to know whether there are overruns or shortfalls. In connection with closing out the budget, special attention will be paid to the latter, but here it is necessary to look at the possibilities implied by the transfer of funds between categories.

Since libraries are budget driven, the intent is to spend the allocated budget properly and profitably. If there are free funds available, say from salary savings, the decision must be made as to where they can best be used. Often such funds are the only source for the purchase of needed equipment, but just as often they can be used to make up for deficiencies in the library materials budget.

The Initial Budget

When the budget is finally committed to paper, it will show not only the amounts allocated to each subject or program, but also any amounts already committed. There will probably also be actual expenditures—e.g., for held-over invoices—but these will not show up as such until the first report from central accounting.

The effect of including encumbrances in the allocation process is clear. Each fund administrator can spend only what is still free. If the allocation has been carried out sensitively, there should be adequate provision for necessary purchases, but when funds are short, it may be necessary to slow down new orders.

There will also be a number of new orders that were held at the end of the previous year. For the most part, they can now be processed. If, however, they are numerous and would reduce the funds available to an undesirable level, it may be necessary to ask the fund administrator to review these orders to determine whether any should be held until it is clearer whether there will be sufficient funds. Such delays should be only a last resort, because the longer orders are held back the more difficult it is to fulfill them.

The initial allocation will also have been based on current serial subscriptions. If possible, decisions should already have been made about cancellations so that these can be deleted when the new preliminary invoice is received from the vendor. Uncertainties about the actual budget or slow responses from selectors may have delayed the process. If so, making such decisions should be among the first steps in actualizing the budget. If some allowance for new subscriptions has been made, these should now be tentatively included—tentatively because their actual cost may not be known until after the vendor receives the order and announces the price. The same reasoning applies to standing orders.

New spending is, therefore, confined to uncommitted funds, mostly for books and other media, and not for long-term commitments.

Encumbering Orders

How to encumber new orders has been the subject of much discussion.[1] The actual price of a book or other one-time purchase is a combination of three factors: the published price, the discount received, and the cost of postage or other dispatch costs. These form an equation:

$$\text{Published price} - \text{discount} + \text{postage} = \text{cost to the library}$$

Of these the one most likely to be known to the library is the published price. Even this is not always as certain as it seems. In France, for example, publishers were forbidden to advertise actual prices. Such ads were seen as restraint of trade, since booksellers could set their own prices. Often also, overseas books must be ordered well in advance of actual publication if they are to be received in a timely manner, and the price may be only tentative or subject to change. The same is true of major sets, printed or microform, whose full price may not be determined until actual completion, or which may be affected by discounts for early ordering. In effect, the published price is becoming equivalent to the "suggested retail price" that shows up so often in discount stores. Nevertheless it offers the surest guide to the likely cost to the library.

Even though discounts may have been negotiated with major vendors, individual books may be subject to different rates of discount; some may have to be purchased at full retail price or even be subject to a surcharge. Books purchased directly from publishers or societies may carry a different range of discounts, and books from small overseas publishers will almost certainly sell at retail price or higher.

The costs of shipping and postage will be borne by the library and cannot be known in advance, since they will vary with the source, the method of dispatch, and the bulk involved.

This suggests that the library is in a bind, but there are several ways of resolving the dilemma. The simplest, and the one that has been used by the author, is to encumber at published price (using a unit price for each subject when no published price is known) and then, to be safe, overencumbering by a percentage that can be tracked from historical records. This is the most suitable way for academic libraries or large public libraries which order many items from a wide range of sources. It can be refined by the use of data gathered from automated accounting and ordering systems.

Some libraries have used such data along with published annual reports to establish unit prices for each subject area. They encumber all purchases on this basis, allowing for more expensive individual items. In such cases the original allocations were also based on unit price. Sampson provides an overview of this kind of process.[2] Where most of a library's purchases are carried out through a cooperative, with established discounts, it is possible to encumber at the discounted price, but even here adjustments will have to be made later to allow for exceptions, or postage, or order processing fees. Whatever the method chosen, the important thing is to be consistent.

Foreign-currency purchases present special problems, particularly with so many floating currencies. Many automated systems, the parent institution, or the local bank can provide lists of exchange rates, and these can be used to calculate dollar prices. They should be updated regularly. Foreign suppliers should be encouraged to invoice and quote in U.S. dollars. This practice simplifies internal bookkeeping and speeds up payments, since such invoices do not have to go through the process of conversion—very important at the end of the year.

Exceptions

There are exceptions to any rule. It is advisable to regard all serial commitments and any projected purchases through blanket orders or approval plans as encumbered at the beginning of the year. They will come in irregularly throughout the year but can be expected to approximate the amount set aside in the budget. Any deviations should be monitored with care to determine their cause.

Another extremely difficult area to predict is the cost of standing orders for sets and continuing irregular publications. Again it is prudent to regard the forward estimates that were used to set up the budget as encumbered, thus preventing the use of apparently unexpended money for other purchases, until it becomes clear whether the original expectations will or will not be met.

Similarly, binding costs are likely to be much in line with those of the previous year, allowing for any price increase and for changes caused by the addition or cancellation of serials. The total should therefore be regarded as encumbered.

Following these rules forestalls the situation in which there may appear to be substantial unused funds and selectors seek to purchase expensive items, only to find that other projected purchases do in fact come in and there is no money left to pay for them.

Recording Payments

When books or other orders are received they will be accompanied by an invoice stating the actual cost to the library. Major vendors should be encouraged to subdivide their invoices by account or fund—particularly when endowment or trust funds are being used. This procedure simplifies the application of invoices to the subdivided library budget, but it is not always possible. The library will then have to suballocate the total cost, prorating discounts and postal charges among the items on the invoice. The simplest of all worlds would be one book, one invoice, but this can apply only in the case of specific individual orders; otherwise the amount of paperwork involved would sink both the library and its suppliers.

Invoices from blanket orders or from approval plans present another kind of difficulty. Most libraries simply set aside funds to cover the expected intake without attempting to subdivide it by subject or fund account. The suppliers may or may not be able to incorporate fund account numbers or similar indications in their invoices. They should, however, be encouraged to do so whenever possible. With automated accounting systems much more common, it is possible to process machine-readable invoices internally and allocate the appropriate amounts to individual funds.

The internal procedure of the library in handling approval plan and similar accounts should have two goals:

1. To be able to assign total expenditures to the appropriate approval plan account.
2. To be able to distribute costs by subject or program, even if these costs were not so distributed in the budget itself.

While such a procedure amounts to setting up a second set of books, it does provide the library with a much fuller report on the distribution of expenditure, making future planning that much easier. The cost can then be compared with the other kind of distribution record, produced by cataloging incoming materials, to see what is happening to the collection as a whole. Such records can be used as evidence that the library is fulfilling its plan and meeting its financial responsibilities.

The same applies to the invoices received from serials vendors, who are usually able to assign fund account numbers to serials or to use a classified distribution. The latter may not always correspond exactly with the library's own categorization, but it can be adapted quite readily. It is vital to be able

to make such assignments of costs, particularly if the library budget allocation is a total one based on all formats combined. Only by assigning costs can
the library determine the effect of differential price increases on the materials budget distribution.

Since the invoice for most serials will be received relatively early in the
July/June budget year, these figures can be used to determine what adjustments must be made, if any. It must be remembered that the initial vendor
invoice may not include all possible charges and that there will be several
instances in which no price is recorded. Allowance can be made for these
omissions by consulting earlier records to determine what kinds of added
costs were received later in the year.

In all cases the procedure for charging involves two steps:

1. The original encumbrance must be liquidated by removing it from
   the account record.
2. The actual cost from the invoice must be charged against the fund
   account in question.

By following this procedure the accounts can be made to reflect actual costs
and expenditures.

A final word of warning: The central accounting office is not concerned
with library subdivisions, only with total budgets and total expenditures.
(The same is true of reserved endowment and special funds, which are
treated as separate budgets.) The central accounting office will simply
charge the amount of the invoice against the appropriate budget line. The
total result is the same, but because of the time lapse in the processing of
invoices, the monthly (or weekly) reports will not correspond with those
kept by the library. This difference must be kept in mind at all times.

Expenditure Patterns

Progress during the year will be irregular, depending on the flow of new
orders, items supplied, and invoices. Most budget officers tend to think of
expenditures as flowing evenly throughout the year, as for example salaries,
and may question low or high expenditures in any period. There are several
reasons why library materials accounts do not follow an even pattern.

First, most libraries will be holding invoices that arrived too late to be
processed in the fiscal year when the order was placed. Unless the institution
follows an accrual accounting procedure, they will now be chargeable against
the new fiscal year. The result is a sudden inflow of expenditures. With any luck
it will not be very large; however, financial problems in the previous year may
have caused the library to hold back a substantial number of invoices.

Second, certain kinds of invoices have patterns of their own. Most serials
vendors, for example, send out renewal invoices early in the fall, expecting
the library to send back adjustments (cancellations and new subscriptions)
before the final invoice is set up and sent for payment. The process may take
a little time, but it finally results in another invoice for a substantial sum. The
total may be modified by an arrangement for a discount for payment before

some specified time. Some institutions do not allow such a procedure, arguing that they can invest the unspent money more profitably, but the savings are usually large enough to allow the library to proceed. The result, of course, is a very substantial payment within the month when it occurs, perhaps as much as 40 percent of the total budget. See figure 9.1.

Other kinds of invoices tend to follow similar patterns—for example, invoices for annual serials, which come around the end of the calendar year. Publishing patterns, with large spring and fall schedules, affect deliveries, particularly on approval plans, and also the timing of individual orders.

Third, in academic libraries, orders placed from faculty suggestions tend to follow the academic year, for example, with a slow start in the summer, peaks at the beginning of each term, and large numbers of suggestions received during slow academic periods, such as January. Course-reserve ordering will also follow term patterns. Most libraries encourage early reserve-reading orders because of the time required to order, receive, and process individual orders. It is wise to allow at least three months for the whole process, but it is also inevitable that many faculty will be late, resulting in a flow of urgent orders for materials that may no longer be available at discounted rates.

Such variations must be explained to budget officers and any other officials who monitor the library budget externally. Their concern, which is a proper one, is with the efficient expenditure of the total budget. They could be misled into thinking that there is a pool of unexpended money available for other uses if they are not made aware of the special patterns involved in

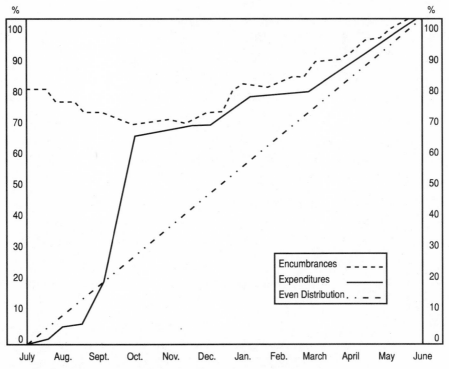

FIGURE 9.1 Library Materials Expenditures over the Budget Year

library expenditures. In reverse, knowing what the library can and cannot do will be useful to them when they are thinking of transfers to the library, or, as is more usual, when thinking of midyear reductions or assessments.

Individual Fund Accounts

Since the purpose of allocating funds is to direct expenditures in accordance with institutional and library priorities, it is necessary to follow carefully their progress within the year. This kind of monitoring is not simply for control but to ensure that objectives are met.[3] The amount expended or encumbered in each account will reflect both the nature of the subject matter and the style of the individual selector. Some are careful to reserve funds for expected peak publishing periods, and others will already have a back list of desirable materials. Progress during the year is likely to be somewhat erratic. Since the goal is to spend the allocated sums, it is essential that selectors be encouraged as far as possible to order high-cost items early in the year—to allow adequate time for delivery. Similarly, foreign materials should be ordered as early as possible.

The effects of blanket-order and approval programs on individual subject selection should be monitored, since it is difficult for the individual selector to be certain what has been covered, whether all presses and publishers are included, and whether there are any price limits on automatic supply. There is always likely to be some overlap, especially in the case of orders originating from faculty requests. These should be handled by the acquisitions staff, either making sure that the requested materials are actually received under the plan or letting the selector know what is not covered.

Selector orders can be useful indicators of failure on the part of the supplier. It is also essential to check up on all reports of nonsupply, such as out of print, not in stock, or reprinting. Studies show that many such reports are inaccurate,[4] and only constant vigilance can ensure that needed materials are actually supplied. The reverse situation can occur when several approval plans are used: it is possible to receive multiple copies of books published simultaneously in more than one country. Provision should be made for the return of such duplicates.

As soon as feasible in the fiscal year, each selector should be encouraged to look at orders for out-of-print materials, sets, and other items likely to take some time either to locate or to obtain. There has been some disagreement on who should decide on the supplier. Usually this is within the control of the acquisitions department, but selectors should be encouraged to search out the best suppliers, particularly for antiquarian items.[5] If feasible, regular reviews of likely dealers should be carried out with each selector.

As the amounts encumbered and spent accumulate, the progress of each fund should be charted. Regular reports to selectors are helpful. These can be quite simple, consisting only of a few lines, as shown in table 9.1.

Where expenditures and encumbrances together indicate that the remaining funds may not be adequate for the rest of the year, the selector should be encouraged to review priorities and to see whether there has been a proper distribution within the subject area. Where the amount expended is lagging behind expectation, the selector should be encouraged to step up

TABLE 9.1   Account Report

Account: English	
Budget	$23,300.00
Spent	17,654.23
Encumbered	3,210.00
Balance	2,435.77

ordering unless there is a valid reason for waiting because of known or expected later publishing. It is entirely possible that, in any given year, there will be a lower amount of publishing than expected or that there are anticipated major publications. Monitoring these situations is a joint task.

Flexibility

Because any budget is simply an educated guess at what is likely to occur over a given year, care should be taken not to be so rigid in controlling fund expenditures that advantage cannot be taken of once-in-a-lifetime opportunities (e.g., a chance to acquire a long-sought antiquarian item or a major reprint set). In the same way, encouraging purchases when there is little to be gained is counterproductive. Flexibility is essential.

Towards the end of the year, it may be possible to reallocate funds or move money from reserved funds to other areas of the budget. On the other hand, it may be necessary to reduce allocations because of some external action (e.g., a general assessment on the budget) or because of unexpected cost increases in other elements (e.g., serial prices or exchange rates). All these situations indicate the need for careful assessment of what is possible and what is most in line with general priorities.

It may be necessary to suspend orders if an individual fund is getting too far ahead of the amount allocated. Even so, allowance has to be made for essential purchases, such as for reserve reading. Another method of control is to ask for a reexamination of priorities on individual requests received. No allocation should be so rigid as to prevent the purchase of important publications. This may be possible only by drawing down reserved funds or using unspent allocations.

Many libraries set a time in the year, usually two to three months before the end of the fiscal year, when all unexpended balances are subject to use for other purchases so that the library will not be left with unexpended funds at a time when it is no longer possible to process orders in time for payment before the end of the fiscal year. Orders received will still be processed, but the primary goal now is not simply to sustain allocations but rather to ensure that the budget is expended.

Different Budget Years

Special funds, such as federal grants, often have different fiscal years; they may also have balances that carry over from year to year, so that matching annual income and expenditure is not always the primary issue. This is a particularly useful characteristic in areas where there are large numbers of antiquarian items or known major purchases for which funds must be allowed to accumulate. Be sure to know the characteristics of each special fund and to judge the relationships of these funds to the general budget.

Financial Reporting

Regular financial reports are essential. At the beginning of the year these are most likely to be monthly, but towards the end of the year they should be provided biweekly or weekly. Not all institutional systems are able to cope with this kind of need, and the library may have to institute an internal reporting system. In such cases internal reports should be carefully reconciled with external reports, since in many cases the latter will lag behind in reporting actual expenditures.

Reports received from central accounting will not agree with library reports for the same period because of the differing ways in which payments are scheduled. There may be a backlog of invoices awaiting processing, or there may be a roster of payment dates for vendors. It is necessary to check each monthly report to see what invoices have been processed.

Some of the problems involved in meshing library accounts with centralized accounting are reviewed by Ellory Christianson, who suggests ways in which the library and the central accounting department can work to resolve these problems.[6] The author recalls having to untangle a logjam caused by having the accounts for the library and various bookstores intertwined within separate vendor accounts to the degree that credits and returns were commingled. As Christianson suggests, it is essential to talk with the accountants in their own language. His article also outlines some of the concerns in establishing linkages between systems. Special care must be paid to the codes used for vendors and for type of transaction. With goodwill on both sides these linkages can be established.

Carol Chamberlain stresses the role that automated acquisitions systems can play in fiscal planning.[7] As with all systems, manual or automated, success depends on good staff and attention to detail. If it is also possible to make use of vendor systems, the result can be a seamless transaction record, but care needs to be taken to ensure compatibility. Moreover, in all libraries some transactions will fall outside any vendor system and, in those libraries which work with multiple vendors, there may be several such systems to consider. Nevertheless, automation has removed much of the chance nature of manual record keeping.

Notes

1. Short treatments of encumbering are provided in Rose Mary Magrill and John Corbin's *Acquisitions Management and Collection Development in Libraries,* 2nd ed. (Chicago: ALA, 1989), pp. 107–8, and in Stephen Ford's *The Acquisition of Library Materials* (Chicago: ALA, 1973), pp. 179–83, 193–94.

2. G. S. Sampson, "Allocating the Book Budget: Measuring Inflation," *College & Research Libraries* 36 (1975): 403–10.

3. Jasper C. Schad, "Allocating Book Funds: Control or Planning," *College & Research Libraries* 31 (1970): 155–59.

4. In a paper presented at the 1991 Charleston Conference, "Books in Limbo," Arlene Moore Sievers (Case Western Reserve University) discussed problems with vendor reports. Her paper will be published by JAI Press. There are also references in the various ALA *Guidelines* and in several of the standard books on acquisitions, but no extended treatment of the subject is available at present.

5. Ronald Ray (Rutgers University) suggested a more cooperative approach to vendor selection in a paper presented at the 1991 Charleston Conference, "Time to Take Selection of Primary Vendors out of Acquisitions and Serials Departments?" This paper will be published by JAI Press.

6. Ellory Christianson, "When Your Parent Dictates Your Accounting Life," *Bottom Line* 7,1 (Summer 1993): 17–21.

7. Carol E. Chamberlain, "Fiscal Planning in Academic Libraries: The Role of Automated Acquisitions Systems," *Advances in Library Organization and Management* 4 (1986): 141–52.

Chapter 10

Budget Adjustments: Midyear Cuts, Assessments, and Budget Additions

In earlier times libraries could feel reasonably certain that the budget as set up at the beginning of the fiscal year would last for that year. The financial problems of many local government and higher education agencies, however, have meant budget shortfalls and requests to cut expenditure. The most common practice has been to impose an across-the-board percentage cut, often called an assessment, which reflects the amount by which expected revenues have fallen short of the initial target.

These cuts may or may not be uniform across the institution and may also be imposed differentially by type of expenditure. For example, unless it is proposed to furlough employees or cut back on their numbers, salary and wage expenditures may be allowed to continue at the same rate. Savings from retirements and other vacancies may be confiscated. Since most governmental activities are labor intensive (perhaps as much as 80 percent of the total budget may be for people or people-related expenditures), all other kinds of expenditures will be assessed more deeply.

Libraries, because of their special patterns of materials expenditures, are particularly affected by these kinds of assessments. Although the response has to be in terms of the whole library, particular attention must be paid to the place library materials expenditure was reached within the year's goals. By late fall most serials payments will probably have been made. Any cut imposed later is likely to affect other kinds of expenditures severely. Standing orders for annuals are likely to come to charge about the end of the calendar year. Unless it is possible (and reasonable) to cancel any of them, they must be accommodated before making any further cuts in allocations. Other standing orders are not easy to cancel and restart; hence they should be seen as encumbered at the beginning of the year.

If the library has approval plans or similar agreements for a regular supply of materials, consideration has to be given to their priority. Changes will require renegotiated profiles or outright cancellation. If they represent a substantial portion of the total budget, immediate consideration must be given to modifications. The decision should be guided by knowledge of whether the cuts are temporary or permanent.

Because finances are no longer stable, many libraries have decided to cut back on approval plans and similar sources of supply.[1] This approach may be somewhat shortsighted, since approval plans are more likely than single item selecting to pick up on individual publications. However, libraries will have to balance the need for comprehensive collecting against the selection of specific needed items. Where a library has an interest in a specific area, the approval plan is more likely to produce a full collection. Such considerations have to be kept in mind when deciding whether to cancel or reduce approval buying.

A severe cut may signal the need for a complete review of library objectives. If the cut is permanent, the library may have to lower its collecting goals or reallocate some funds to access or buying-on-demand document delivery. Any library faced with a permanent budget reduction will have to look very hard at its permanent commitments as represented by serials and standing orders. Many libraries have experienced the need to reduce serials expenditure and conduct annual reviews of subscriptions. The farther ahead this can be planned, the easier it is to accommodate budget cuts. In most cases, review during the final quarter of the fiscal year will enable libraries to react more effectively to budget reductions or to later assessments.

Another kind of reduction may be the decision to cut certain kinds of expenditures entirely. Public libraries, for example, may decide that it is not possible to maintain an acceptable level of video purchases, particularly since there are other ways that users can obtain videos. Complete elimination of audiovisuals may have deleterious effects in certain subject fields or in services to the elderly or hearing impaired, and cuts would have to be balanced by drawing on regional resources.

In an academic setting, such services are often shared among agencies, and a new distribution of responsibilities may be needed. Also it may be possible to redirect users to other institutions or agencies, for example for foreign newspapers. However, there are limits to how far service-sharing can be carried, since all other agencies face the same kinds of problems. It is useful to determine what other parts of the institution carry similar materials. There may be a newspaper-reading room for language students or for various ethnic-studies organizations.

It may be possible to rationalize collecting or to arrange for the library to hold archival copies. Most such solutions take time, and the library may have to make quick decisions about what to do in the short run. Here, knowledge of what else is happening within the institution or any surrounding libraries will be of assistance. If the institution has been allowing individual departments to purchase materials for departmental use, now may be the time to ask for a review of this policy. Of particular interest are library materials acquired from grant money when the library is already buying them for general use.

Much of the library's response will be determined by the urgency of the central request. If time is allowed for consultation, it is easier to make appropriate decisions. Mostly, however, the financial situation is such that there is no time for consultation. The library must simply make the best decision it can and seek to improve the situation later.

Library Use as a Factor

When adjusting budgets to meet cutbacks, knowledge of actual use can be an important tool. If certain collections are less used than others, they can survive greater reductions. Care must be taken, however, not to look at usage simplistically. Some areas, such as reference collections, do not circulate, and internal usage records may be inadequate. The records for others may reflect cyclical usage—e.g., courses may not be taught every year—while yet others may have archival or national significance.

In such areas the loss of acquisitions during one or more years may cause added pressures in later years to fill perceived gaps. It is difficult to defend collections which are only marginal locally but which represent significant resources for the larger community, but, unless the library can manage such a defense, all libraries will suffer. Here emphasis can be laid on the benefits to the local community of access to other collections which complement the local collections.

Reference collections need continuous support because outdated reference tools are worse than no tools at all. There have been many short articles in the library press on the problems of outdated encyclopedias in schools, or on the difficulties of working with old issues of manuals.[2] This kind of response can be extended to almost all kinds of reference works. Bad or inadequate information is worse than no information. Now that it is becoming more and more possible to obtain specific materials (articles or books on interlibrary loan or via document delivery) it has become increasingly important to have the best locating tools, whether in print or on-line format.

These situations suggest some of the considerations that must be taken into account when responding to budget cuts. Unless the library is careful to foresee the long-term effects, one year's cuts may be reflected over many years in poorer library service to users. The author, leading a library assessment team, was reminded forcibly by several faculty members that low buying rates over a couple of decades had impoverished the collections to a level that certain kinds of research were impossible using only local resources and that borrowing from other libraries was both costly and time consuming, given the basic nature of the works involved. This need is not always clear to administrators, who seldom undertake such research. It is too easy to say that reliance can always be placed on resource sharing. The fact is that other libraries were probably also affected by the same financial stringency, and many resource-sharing plans were vitiated by the inability of the participants to guarantee adequate total coverage.

Library Response to Budget Cuts

The nature of the individual library's response will be, in large measure, dictated by the rules set by the parent institution. These rules may specify what budget areas will be cut and to what degree. If the library has laid a good groundwork of understanding with those responsible for budget control, it may be asked to bear only a lower level of reduction or given more time to meet specified goals. Another possibility is wider latitude in the transfer of unspent money between budget lines (or programs). Much of this resource will represent either salary savings or money for other projected expenditures such as equipment or furniture. Here the library has to decide which objective is the more desirable, and the decision may not always come down on the side of library materials.[3]

Any individual library may also decide that it is possible to postpone a specific program, for example reclassification or record conversion, or it may be possible to seek noninstitutional funds.

A further option is the transfer of regular budget expenditures to special funds. Here care has to be taken that the purposes of the original grant or endowment are not overturned. If funds were given with the expectation that they were to be used for the enrichment of the collection or to meet needs not covered by the regular budget, such a transfer may not be possible. In many cases, however, it is permissible to transfer not only future obligations but past expenditures, and doing so may enable the library to meet its ongoing commitments without undue hardship. When the library must report back on specific purchases or use gift plates, retrospective transfers are impossible.

One other factor should be borne in mind. Such transfers may encourage the parent institution to make temporary cuts permanent because the library seems to have other sources of income. Care also has to be taken that they do not change drastically the distribution of expenditure. Some counterbalancing action may have to be taken in later years to make up for temporary losses.

Most libraries do not have extensive reserves and will simply have to cut back on planned expenditures. What might happen in such a situation is set out in the following tables: first, in tables 10.1 and 10.2, which show actual

TABLE 10.1   Library Materials Budget
Academic Library
Expenditure Midyear

Area	Books	Standing Orders	Serials	Data-bases	Media	Micro-forms	Totals
REFERENCE							
General	$ 1,100	$ 2,900	$14,500	$11,000	$ 600	$ 500	$ 30,600
Fine Arts	950	1,600	9,370	3,000	500	—	15,420
Humanities	2,650	3,900	15,000	9,100	—	—	30,650
Science	3,200	4,000	22,010	11,000	—	—	40,210
Social Science	1,600	1,800	5,910	7,500	—	—	16,810
Technology	960	1,200	3,310	6,200	—	—	11,670
Subtotal	10,460	15,400	70,100	47,800	1,100	500	145,360
GENERAL							
Documents	4,300	—	2,100	—	—	2,100	8,500
General	13,000	2,150	16,200	—	—	3,000	34,350
Professional	600	600	1,750	—	—	—	2,950
Replacements	6,200	—	—	—	—	—	6,200
Subtotal	24,100	2,750	20,050	0	0	5,100	52,000

(continued)

TABLE 10.1   *(continued)*

Area	Books	Standing Orders	Serials	Data-bases	Media	Micro-forms	Totals
FINE ARTS							
Art History	$ 6,210	$ 750	$ 3,020	$ —	$ 1,200	$ 1,000	$ 12,180
Music	2,905	3,410	1,900	—	—	—	8,215
Professional Arts	2,600	400	3,000	—	10,100	—	16,100
Subtotal	11,715	4,560	7,920	0	11,300	1,000	36,495
HUMANITIES							
Classics	2,100	600	2,490	—	—	—	5,190
English	12,650	700	3,210	—	0	—	16,560
Modern Languages	8,750	650	4,680	—	1,100	—	15,180
Philosophy	3,970	650	4,730	—	—	—	9,350
Subtotal	27,470	2,600	15,110	0	1,100	0	46,280
SCIENCE							
Biology	2,680	4,970	85,550	—	800	—	94,000
Chemistry	2,100	6,250	89,100	—	—	—	97,450
Computer Science	1,510	890	7,680	—	—	—	10,080
Mathematics	1,750	3,960	33,310	—	—	—	39,020
Physics	1,615	1,900	86,950	—	—	—	90,465
Subtotal	9,655	17,970	302,590	0	800	0	331,015
SOCIAL SCIENCES							
Economics	3,950	610	11,970	—	—	—	16,530
Education	2,715	590	9,760	—	1,500	1,700	16,265
History	9,620	800	15,100	—	490	2,600	28,610
Political Science	4,250	310	11,250	—	—	—	15,810
Psychology	4,790	795	21,010	—	—	—	26,595
Sociology	6,995	510	10,520	—	795	2,750	21,570
Subtotal	32,320	3,615	79,610	0	2,785	7,050	125,380
TECHNOLOGY (Engineering)							
General	1,210	510	11,950	—	750	—	14,420
Chemical	1,000	205	14,575	—	—	—	15,780
Civil	2,650	1,510	12,640	—	500	—	17,300
Design	975	110	5,680	—	800	—	7,565
Electrical	625	600	17,795	—	—	—	19,020
Mechanical	2,720	715	27,210	—	—	—	30,645
Subtotal	9,180	3,650	89,850	0	2,050	0	104,730
BINDING							29,760
GRAND TOTAL	124,900	50,545	585,230	47,800	19,135	13,650	871,020
PERCENTAGE OF TOTAL	14.34%	5.80%	67.19%	5.49%	2.20%	1.57%	100.00%
ORIGINAL ALLOCATION	225,750	78,850	591,900	48,000	31,300	21,700	1,050,000
FREE BALANCE	100,850	28,305	6,670	200	12,165	8,050	178,900

expenditures and encumbrances to date; and then in tables 10.3 and 10.4, which show how it might be possible to adapt the existing budget to an overall reduction of 10 percent. By the middle of the year an academic library will already have spent virtually all the amount set aside for serials. Because many

TABLE 10.2   Library Materials Budget
Public Library
Expenditure Midyear

Area	Books	Standing Orders	Serials	Data-bases	Media	Total	Percentage of Total
REFERENCE	$ 7,635	$ 9,250	$ 5,100	$13,950	$ 250	$ 36,185	19.31%
ADULT							
Nonfiction	25,000	0	0	0	2,700	27,700	14.78%
Business	2,100	1,750	3,525	3,150	500	11,025	5.88%
Careers	1,100	450	1,975	1,970	600	6,095	3.25%
Periodicals	0	0	56,120	0	0	56,120	29.95%
Audiovisuals	0	0	0	0	6,250	6,250	3.34%
Gen. Fiction	16,250	0	0	0	0	16,250	8.67%
Mystery	1,300	0	0	0	0	1,300	0.69%
Romance	1,575	0	0	0	0	1,575	0.84%
Paperbacks	1,300	0	0	0	0	1,300	0.69%
Rental	[6,500]	0	0	0	0	[6,500]	
Large Print	2,000	0	0	0	0	2,000	1.07%
Subtotal	50,625	2,200	61,620	5,120	10,050	129,615	69.18%
YOUNG ADULT							
Nonfiction	1,720	0	615	0	0	2,335	1.25%
Fiction	3,550	0	0	0	0	3,550	1.89%
Audiovisuals	0	0	0	0	2,300	2,300	1.23%
Subtotal	5,270	0	615	0	2,300	8,185	4.37%
CHILDREN							
Reference	1,400	0	1,150	2,250	0	4,800	2.56%
Nonfiction	1,550	0	0	0	0	1,550	0.83%
Fiction	2,750	0	0	0	0	2,750	1.47%
Picture Books	3,575	0	0	0	0	3,575	1.91%
Audiovisuals	0	0	0	0	700	700	0.37%
Subtotal	9,275	0	1,150	2,250	700	13,375	7.14%
GRAND TOTAL	72,805	11,450	68,485	21,320	13,300	187,360	100.00%
PERCENTAGE OF TOTAL	38.86%	6.11%	36.55%	11.38%	7.10%	100.00%	
ORIGINAL ALLOCATION	130,600	21,000	67,100	21,700	22,100	262,500	
FREE BALANCE	57,795	9,550	(1,385)	380	8,800	75,410	

standing orders are for annuals, a significant proportion of the expenditure in this category will fall in the January–March period. This outlay must still be allowed for unless it is possible at this date to cancel existing orders. Database expenditures are usually serial in nature and paid up front. Cancellations and refunds are possible but unlikely. Expenditures for media and microforms will vary with the nature of the planned purchase. Some will be for major sets and were probably initiated early in the year. Unspent funds may also have been set aside to cover successive parts of sets.

These facts leave only the "book" allocation available for significant reductions. Where cuts can be made, and their nature, will depend on expenditures and outstanding orders to date. Unless substantial funds can be salvaged from other budget areas, most subject allocations will have to be severely reduced, even to the degree that no further orders can be placed. It is worth noting that the library has already reached a point where it could not meet a 20 percent cut.

A possible response is shown in table 10.3. Here most cuts have been made in books and by postponing some binding. This is largely because the orders for serials and standing orders are firm orders and cannot be cancelled. This is an emergency response, but, unless the cuts are likely to be restored in succeeding years, successive budgets will have to be recast drastically.

Other variations are possible. These can include reductions in program expenditure or the transfer of some amounts to access budgets. Whatever the

TABLE 10.3 Library Materials Budget
Academic Library
10 Percent Budget Cut

Area	Books	Standing Orders	Serials	Data-bases	Media	Micro-forms	Totals
REFERENCE							
General	$ 2,000	$ 5,700	$ 15,100	$11,000	$ 600	$ 500	$ 34,900
Fine Arts	1,800	2,200	9,800	3,000	500	—	17,300
Humanities	3,500	5,900	15,750	9,100	—	—	34,250
Science	4,750	7,800	22,300	11,000	—	—	45,850
Social Science	3,500	2,800	6,000	7,500	—	—	19,800
Technology	1,800	2,300	3,650	6,200	—	—	13,950
Subtotal	17,350	26,700	72,600	47,800	1,100	500	166,050
GENERAL							
Documents	8,000	—	3,000	—	—	2,100	13,100
General	24,600	6,000	18,000	—	—	6,000	54,600
Professional	1,500	1,100	2,100	—	—	—	4,700
Replacements	9,250	—	—	—	—	—	9,250
Subtotal	43,350	7,100	23,100	0	0	8,100	81,650
FINE ARTS							
Art History	10,500	1,000	3,500	—	1,500	1,000	17,500
Music	5,500	4,900	2,100	—	—	—	12,500
Professional Arts	4,160	550	3,300	—	14,000	—	22,010
Subtotal	20,160	6,450	8,900	0	15,500	1,000	52,010
HUMANITIES							
Classics	4,510	1,000	3,100	—	—	—	8,610
English	22,900	1,550	4,300	—	0	—	28,750
Modern Languages	14,000	1,800	6,000	—	1,200	—	23,000
Philosophy	7,600	650	5,450	—	—	—	13,700
Subtotal	49,010	5,000	18,850	0	1,200	0	74,060
SCIENCE							
Biology	2,900	6,500	86,000	—	800	—	96,200
Chemistry	2,350	8,700	89,100	—	—	—	100,150
Computer Science	1,900	1,000	7,680	—	—	—	10,580
Mathematics	2,200	4,400	35,400	—	—	—	42,000
Physics	2,050	2,100	87,000	—	—	—	91,150
Subtotal	11,400	22,700	305,180	0	800	0	340,080

TABLE 10.3   *(continued)*

Area	Books	Standing Orders	Serials	Data-bases	Media	Micro-forms	Totals
SOCIAL SCIENCES							
Economics	$ 8,600	$ 730	$ 11,970	$ —	$ —	$ —	$ 21,300
Education	5,300	1,000	9,760	—	1,600	1,700	19,360
History	17,000	1,000	15,650	—	500	2,600	36,750
Political Science	8,700	500	11,250	—	—	—	20,450
Psychology	8,000	800	21,010	—	—	—	29,810
Sociology	13,000	655	10,520	—	800	2,750	27,725
Subtotal	60,600	4,685	80,160	0	2,900	7,050	155,395
TECHNOLOGY (Engineering)							
General	1,600	540	11,950	—	850	—	14,940
Chemical	1,600	540	14,575	—	—	—	16,715
Civil	3,100	2,100	12,640	—	900	—	18,740
Design	1,350	110	5,680	—	900	—	8,040
Electrical	1,000	600	17,795	—	—	—	19,395
Mechanical	3,500	715	27,210	—	—	—	31,425
Subtotal	12,150	4,605	89,850	0	2,650	0	109,255
BINDING							50,500
GRAND TOTAL	214,020	77,240	598,640	47,800	24,150	16,650	1,029,000
PERCENTAGE OF TOTAL	20.80%	7.51%	58.18%	4.65%	2.35%	1.62%	100.00%
ORIGINAL ALLOCATION	225,750	78,850	591,900	48,000	31,300	21,700	

resulting changes, the library will have to reassess its approach to collecting, whether to recoup its losses or to make permanent a different approach to resource management. If such budget changes extend over two or more years, the library may well have to restructure its entire budget.

Public libraries usually have a lower proportion of their budgets assigned to serials and similar committed expenditures. Nevertheless, payments for such orders will already have been made, thus reducing the areas available for adjustment. The midyear situation is shown in table 10.2. The library's response to the cut must include reviews of all programs. In this case, both the business and career projects are in the special situation of having outside funding and needing to be maintained to continue eligibility for that funding. Library usage can provide a guide as to where cuts can be made. A further consideration is that many audiovisual materials are available from other sources, but *not* most nonfiction titles or titles intended for the handicapped. Such considerations limit to some extent what the library can cut.

A possible response is shown in table 10.4. This shows reductions principally in adult fiction and nonfiction expenditures and in most audiovisual allocations. Again it is worth noting that the library has already passed the 80 percent expenditure mark, largely because of early payments for serials and quasiserials.

TABLE 10.4   Library Materials Budget
Public Library
10 Percent Budget Cut

Area	Books	Standing Orders	Serials	Data-bases	Media	Total	Percentage of Total
REFERENCE	$ 8,240	$17,500	$ 5,100	$14,400	$ 300	$ 45,540	19.28%
ADULT							
Nonfiction	37,500	0	0	0	2,800	40,300	17.06%
Business	3,900	2,450	3,525	3,200	800	13,875	5.87%
Careers	1,900	500	2,000	2,000	700	7,100	3.01%
Periodicals	0	0	56,000	0	0	56,000	23.70%
Audiovisuals	0	0	0	0	7,250	7,250	3.07%
Gen. Fiction	27,100	0	0	0	0	27,100	11.47%
Mystery	2,000	0	0	0	0	2,000	0.85%
Romance	2,000	0	0	0	0	2,000	0.85%
Paperbacks	2,000	0	0	0	0	2,000	0.85%
Rental	[6,500]		0	0	0	[6,500]	
Large Print	3,250	0	0	0	0	3,250	1.38%
Subtotal	79,650	2,950	61,525	5,200	11,550	160,875	68.10%
YOUNG ADULT							
Nonfiction	2,800	0	600	0	0	3,400	1.44%
Fiction	5,500	0	0	0	0	5,500	2.33%
Audiovisuals	0	0	0	0	2,600	2,600	1.10%
Subtotal	8,300	0	600	0	2,600	11,500	4.87%
CHILDREN							
Reference	2,200	0	1,100	2,100	0	5,400	2.29%
Nonfiction	2,100	0	0	0	0	2,100	0.89%
Fiction	4,085	0	0	0	0	4,085	1.73%
Picture Books	5,750	0	0	0	0	5,750	2.43%
Audiovisuals	0	0	0	0	1,000	1,000	0.42%
Subtotal	14,135	0	1,100	2,100	1,000	18,335	7.76%
GRAND TOTAL	110,325	20,450	68,325	21,700	15,450	236,250	100.00%
PERCENTAGE OF TOTAL	46.70%	8.66%	28.92%	9.19%	6.54%	100.00%	
ORIGINAL ALLOCATION	130,600	21,000	67,100	21,700	22,100		

Budget Additions

Although the experience is increasingly rare, many libraries have found themselves faced with quite a different problem: how to cope with budget additions late in the year. Institutions are also budget driven, and when it appears that some expenditures will be below the projected levels, they will seek ways to expend funds before the end of the budget year. Many will try to purchase expensive equipment or to replace furniture and other capital assets, but there are limits to what can be done in this way because of the lead time involved. They may turn to the library as a way of using unexpended funds. Some institutions have a long history of such strategies; others seem simply to take the easiest way out.

One example is provided by the experience of the Auburn University libraries. Here the president decided the library would have first call on unspent funds, and Nancy Gibbs describes the benefits and problems inherent in such an approach.[4] Once again the important factor is the understanding between the library and the administration regarding what the library can and cannot do. Spending large sums of money in a short time requires several antecedent factors: a library plan, adequate records, properly controlled back files of orders, or a backup plan for special orders. It also requires clear understandings with the library's suppliers.

Windfall funds can often be used to benefit greatly both the library and the institution. However, unless there is an adequate plan, much of the money can easily be wasted on readily accessible materials. Quite apart from buying new materials, say a microform set or a major reprint, it is possible to use the new money to pay in advance for known future expenditures such as depository accounts or approval plans. Care needs to be taken here to see that such expenditures are both necessary and acceptable within the institution's accounting guidelines. Paying institutional dues in advance may be acceptable, but not payment for materials not yet delivered. Deposits for government documents may be appropriate, but not three-year renewals on serials. In any event, records must be kept of such advance payments since they affect the next year's accounts. They can be used effectively to even out variations in funding but should not be used to change the intentions of the budgetary authority.

The possibility of taking care of overdue binding or repair work should not be overlooked. Not all binders can handle a sudden influx of work, and they should be consulted first. It may be possible to substitute a special shipment for a regular one, or perhaps to send out reference binding that would otherwise have had to wait for the lower use period of the summer.

As with budget cuts, unexpected windfalls will have different impacts, depending on when they are received. If they are late in the budget year, it may be impossible to order materials and have them received before the annual billing period expires, and so advance payments may be the only possible recourse. With adequate advance warning, regular purchases can be made, even if they require a trip to the vendor or to bookstores outside the local area. Good relationships with vendors help in such situations. Another possibility is the rapid review of catalogs from dealers and publishers. Now that electronic communications are more common, it is easier to send in bulk orders with some assurance of prompt supply.

Like budget cuts, budget additions often carry the assumption that the library has no preexistent plan and that any money can be used effectively. Insofar as most libraries have want lists, this is true, but sudden infusions of money can only be used to purchase readily available materials, which may not actually be high on the library's priority list. The library must, in these circumstances, be willing to bend its priorities, but it should not simply buy easily purchased materials if they are not likely to be used.

It is desirable that every library should have a contingency plan. A plan of this kind should note collection areas in need of enhancement or replacement because of condition. It should also refer to any buildup of back orders for antiquarian materials. Here again, however, quick purchase may not be possible, or it may require such extraordinary measures as visiting dealers, lists in hand. Good relationships with dealers will help, and many can send lists of titles or subject catalogs to aid in selection.

Notes

1. Martin Warzala, "The Evolution of Approval Services," *Library Trends* 42,3 (Winter 1994): 514–23.

2. Sherman Hayes, in "Budgeting for and Controlling the Cost of *Other* in Library Expenditure: The Distant Relative in the Budgetary Process," in *Financial Planning for Libraries,* edited by Murray S. Martin (New York: Haworth, 1983), pp. 121–31, provides an excellent overview of the "other" category of the budget and some of the ways in which it can best be exploited.

3. "The Smaller Library," *Bottom Line* 7,2 (Fall 1993): 5, discusses the Warehouse Point Library.

4. Nancy Gibbs, "It's Hard Work Spending Money: Handling Budget Aberrations," in *Proceedings, Conference on Acquisitions, Budgets, and Collections,* compiled and edited by David C. Genaway (Canfield, Ohio: Genaway and Associates, 1991), pp. 113–22.

Chapter 11

Closing Out the Library Materials Budget

The process of closing out the budget includes not only tying down loose ends and making sure that all invoices on hand have been processed, but also the lead-in period needed to achieve those ends. For this reason preparations for completing the budget year should begin at least three months before its nominal close. In most instances that will mean April. It takes sixty to ninety days to complete a purchase and a week or more to process the paperwork. If too many actions are left until the last minute, some of the invoices may not be processed, and the budget will be underspent.

At the end of March (or the appropriate month if the budget year does not end in June) all accounts should be reviewed to see what has been spent, what is encumbered, and what free balances remain. All budget areas will be in the same situation, and there should be constant intercommunication among those responsible. They should work to ensure that the best possible use is made of unspent funds.

Review the previous year's records to see what late adjustments occurred. For instance, there may have been price adjustments for serials or late arrivals on standing orders. These are likely to recur, and funds will be needed to meet them.

Were there any sudden influxes on approval plans resulting from spring publishing schedules? Is the same pattern likely?

Was there a rush of orders for summer reserve reading, or early orders for the fall semester?

Are there any unusual conditions surrounding outstanding orders— say, a postal strike—especially with foreign orders?

The answers to these and similar questions will help determine how far to go in placing regular orders.

At this stage, review each fund account with the responsible selector to determine whether there are any backlogs, major purchases, or difficulties in finding appropriate materials. The approach will vary with the condition of the fund in question. Some will be heavily encumbered, some will be almost spent out, and others will still have funds to spare. Now is the time to decide whether a fund can be allowed to exceed its budget, or whether to hold back all but essential orders. There is no point in adhering to a preset budget if it is unlikely to result in the full expenditure of allocated funds.

Now is also a proper time to consider whether funds can be reallocated, as was discussed earlier in relation to special collections and major sets. In part such decisions will depend on other library and institutional decisions. If there are free funds from salary savings or because planned major equipment purchases did not come to pass, the library administration will have to decide how these can best be used. It may be in the library's best interest to replace worn-out equipment or to invest in new electronic equipment. The latter may, indeed, become a joint project if the decision is to go ahead with the purchase of a CD-ROM work station and databases to use on it.

On the other hand it may be that other areas of the library are overspent (for valid reasons, such as an externally imposed pay increase or a hike in fees) and need access to unspent funds from elsewhere in the budget. Priorities should be set as quickly as possible to allow the time needed for processing orders.

Once fund reallocations have been planned, selectors should be encouraged to expend any balances rapidly. Prompt action is particularly important if the library has been overencumbering so as to allow for expected discounts as discussed previously. Now is the time to review want lists for expensive items that can be purchased readily. Less attention can be paid to meeting the constraints of the original allocations and more to spending the remaining funds profitably.

Every week, outstanding orders should be reviewed and the likely time for their receipt estimated. Calls to dealers will often enable the librarian to find out whether large orders are on the way—for example, from standing orders or approval plans. Each month the account balances should be reviewed for progress. It may also be necessary to check with publishers concerning dealer status reports, since publishers often have small stocks of older titles which are not made available to dealers[1] or may recently have decided on a reprint or a new print run. In some cases dealer orders will need to be cancelled and direct orders placed. In others, paperbacks can be substituted for hardback titles. These tasks are time consuming, but they help the library to meet both its selecting objectives and its financial goals. Choosing between alternatives may be difficult, but that is how to determine the best way to spend funds.

Institutional Constraints

Most kinds of payments have set cutoff times. These may be quite early for major items which require prior approval—for example, such capital equipment items as CD-ROM work stations and items purchased by another institutional agency, such as furniture. An early deadline is often set for invoices in foreign currencies, since these must clear a banking process to determine dollar amount before payment can be made. Not only may there be different schedules for different kinds of payments, but there may also be a sequence (usually alphabetical) in which invoices are processed. Credits and refunds may also get different treatment; they may be processed together with invoices or set off against other payments to the same vendor. Being aware of these procedures enables the library to process invoices in ways most likely to ensure payment by the proper time.

The final cutoff time also varies. Some institutions insist on having all invoices in and paid by the last day of the fiscal year. Others allow various periods of grace ranging from as little as three days to several weeks. Grace periods allow for the inevitable accumulation of late invoices as the various parts of the institution attempt to close out their own budgets.

One specific item will be of concern to libraries. The annual meeting of the American Library Association takes place late in June. Sometimes it runs over into July. If that happens, institutions which will not accept invoices after the end of the fiscal year, even for costs incurred during that year, will require that such costs be held over. Travel expenses associated with attending the meeting will fall into the next fiscal year. Unless the budget initially allowed for two annual meeting expenses, there may well be an underexpenditure of travel funds in one year and an overexpenditure in another, which in turn will affect other budget categories.

The instructions may also allow for the processing of final paychecks, but here libraries should be aware that part-time or hourly workers' final payments may not be posted to the fiscal year's budget if the end of the year does not coincide with a regular pay date. The resulting carryover may change the distribution of funds considerably unless the library has prepared adequately.

Final Closeout Period

The last few weeks of the fiscal year can be extremely difficult. Everyone is trying to process last-minute invoices, and the central accounting office will probably not be able to run budget checks readily. Many automated accounting systems provide only for regularly scheduled budget runs and cannot accommodate special requests—certainly not at the busiest time of the year. For the library this can be very awkward, since it is then impossible to know what invoices have actually been paid and what balances are left.

During the last month the library will have to be guided by educated guesses built on past experience. Internal accounting programs can help, but they cannot show the state of the central records. At this time, the library will need to look at various procedures not ordinarily used, with a view to using funds effectively. In an account with plenty of assets, forward payments may be made to vendors or to depository accounts. If a large invoice is received for an account which cannot accommodate it, it may be possible to transfer it to another account. Within the general library materials budget, one allocation may be spent and another have plenty of funds but little likelihood of receiving new invoices. Rather than try to maintain the original allocations, it would be wise to allow overexpenditure in accounts that have invoices ready for processing and not hold them back in the hope that the undercommitted allocations will still receive invoices. If there have been troubles with some invoices, such as part supply or some wrong items, see if the vendor can supply an amended invoice for the items correctly supplied. Avoid, if possible, credit notes late in the year. These will almost certainly cause problems in central accounting. Instead, ask vendors to hold them for later processing.

Again it is necessary to emphasize that all those concerned with library accounts must cooperate. The goal is not to protect turf but to make the best use of the library budget. Outstanding orders for any part of the budget need to be watched, and the fiscal officer of the library should make sure that all are aware of the current state of the budget. That officer also needs to be aware of controls or restraints on transfers within the budget or between budgets and of rules regarding forward payments or deposits.

Decisions about the transfer of funds will be affected by the ease with which any resulting invoices (or purchases resulting in invoices) can be processed. If the time for approval of capital expenditures has passed, it is no use attempting to buy new equipment. In this setting, supplies or library material items are the easiest to acquire quickly. Stocking up on bar-code labels may be the most profitable way of preparing for the next year and freeing some of next year's funds for other purposes. Buying readily available large sets may be possible, but delivery is not always as prompt as promised unless the library is willing to pay extra for rush delivery.

The author is reminded of a state institution which had been able over a number of years to acquire the entire set of reprints of the British Colonial Office records with year-end funds. They made a fine appearance on the shelves but were rarely, if ever, used. Such purchases may be very tempting, fiscally speaking, but are counterproductive in collection-management terms. More appropriate would be the replacement of heavily used dictionaries or encyclopedias. In the last resort the librarian may decide to visit local bookstores to purchase second copies of heavily used titles or to acquire discounted items. The intention of this section is not to encourage foolish spending but to point out that there are ways of spending money that do not vitiate library goals. Nancy Gibbs provides some excellent pointers.[2]

Year-End Report

As soon as the fiscal year has closed, prepare a report on library materials expenditures as shown by the library's own accounts. This will serve as the base against which to check institutional reports. Most institutions prepare several preliminary reports to allow budget or fiscal officers to check them for accuracy.

Errors may include application to the wrong account or even the wrong budget and may also include payments that should have been applied to other agencies. More important, however, is the detailed list of payments, which enables the librarian to see what invoices were actually processed and whether they were correctly applied. Generating such a list may take some internal adjusting, since few central accounting systems allow for the subdivisions employed by libraries. The first goal is to see whether the totals agree. If not, it may be necessary to confer with the central accounting office to determine whether any remedial action can be taken. The second is to see whether the distribution aimed at by the library was achieved. This task takes rather more time and cannot be completed until the final run of the year-end statement is received.

When the final figures have been settled, it is time to prepare a report for internal distribution. Tables 11.1 and 11.2 show such reports. As can be seen, the general goals were met, but there are some variations. Fund accounts dependent on foreign purchases show the effects of slow delivery and currency fluctuations. Price increases in some areas were greater than anticipated, and in others publishing lagged so that fewer items than expected were supplied. Areas such as standing orders can be expected to show deviations in both directions because this kind of publishing is usually irregular. This report will form the basis for the next year's allocations, since it will show whether further adjustments must be made for inflation and what amounts are represented by outstanding encumbrances.

TABLE 11.1   Library Materials Budget
Academic Library
Year-End Expenditure
(Preliminary)

Area	Books	Standing Orders	Serials	Data-bases	Media	Micro-forms	Totals	Percentage of Total	Amount Encumbered
REFERENCE									
General	$ 2,720	$ 6,510	$15,150	$11,200	$ 1,100	$ 1,100	$ 37,780	3.57%	$ 570
Fine Arts	1,750	2,610	9,470	3,200	1,100	—	18,130	1.71%	110
Humanities	3,710	5,620	15,250	9,200	—	—	33,780	3.19%	875
Science	4,760	8,130	24,020	10,800	—	—	47,710	4.50%	220
Social Science	2,970	3,150	5,610	7,600	—	—	19,330	1.82%	165
Technology	1,850	2,300	3,430	6,300	—	—	13,880	1.31%	220
Subtotal	17,760	28,320	72,930	48,300	2,200	1,100	170,610	16.10%	2,160
GENERAL									
Documents	7,960	—	3,470	—	—	2,200	13,630	1.29%	40
General	22,700	5,600	18,520	—	—	8,900	55,720	5.26%	575
Professional	1,600	1,970	2,200	—	—	—	5,770	0.54%	55
Replacements	10,760	—	—	—	—	—	10,760	1.02%	250
Subtotal	43,020	7,570	24,190	0	0	11,100	85,880	8.11%	920
FINE ARTS									
Art History	10,970	1,000	3,300	—	2,000	1,000	18,270	1.72%	175
Music	5,800	5,700	2,250	—	—	—	13,750	1.30%	250
Performing Arts	4,525	300	3,100	—	14,500	—	22,425	2.12%	530
Subtotal	21,295	7,000	8,650	0	16,500	1,000	54,445	5.14%	955
HUMANITIES									
Classics	4,700	795	3,180	—	—	—	8,675	0.82%	150
English	22,950	1,710	4,500	—	1,150	—	30,310	2.86%	1310
Modern Languages	15,180	2,010	6,110	—	2,300	—	25,600	2.42%	655
Philosophy	7,850	315	5,330	—	—	—	13,495	1.27%	150
Subtotal	50,680	4,830	19,120	0	3,450	0	78,080	7.37%	2,325

(continued)

TABLE 11.1 *(continued)*

Area	Books	Standing Orders	Serials	Data-bases	Media	Micro-forms	Totals	Percentage of Total	Amount Encumbered
SCIENCE									
Biology	$ 2,610	$ 6,500	$ 87,030	—$	1,000 $	— $	97,140	9.17%	$ 410
Chemistry	1,975	9,600	89,600	—	—	—	101,175	9.55%	75
Computer									
Science	2,395	1,200	7,450	—	—	—	11,045	1.04%	55
Mathematics	2,620	4,325	34,900	—	—	—	41,845	3.95%	65
Physics	2,300	2,360	88,700	—	—	—	93,360	8.81%	70
Subtotal	11,900	23,985	307,680	0	1,000	0	344,565	32.52%	675
SOCIAL SCIENCES									
Economics	9,250	640	12,030	—	—	—	21,920	2.07%	260
Education	5,760	1,210	10,250	—	2,640	1,425	21,285	2.01%	305
History	18,015	970	16,010	—	400	4,350	39,745	3.75%	255
Political Science	8,890	220	11,670	—	—	—	20,780	1.96%	370
Psychology	8,800	980	22,015	—	—	—	31,795	3.00%	165
Sociology	14,050	525	9,760	—	1,210	2,875	28,420	2.68%	285
Subtotal	64,765	4,545	81,735	0	4,250	8,650	163,945	15.47%	1,640
TECHNOLOGY (Engineering)									
General	1,600	420	11,815	—	1,000	—	14,835	1.40%	110
Chemical	1,875	570	14,650	—	—	—	17,095	1.61%	175
Civil	3,290	2,305	12,400	—	900	—	18,895	1.78%	110
Design	1,705	100	6,000	—	1,400	—	9,205	0.87%	55
Electrical	1,210	590	17,870	—	—	—	19,670	1.86%	75
Mechanical	3,210	580	26,250	—	—	—	30,040	2.84%	75
Subtotal	12,890	4,565	88,985	0	3,300	0	109,740	10.36%	600
BINDING							52,300	4.94%	
GRAND TOTAL	222,310	80,815	603,290	48,300	30,700	21,850	1,059,565	100.00%	9,275
PERCENTAGE OF TOTAL	20.98%	7.63%	56.94%	4.56%	2.90%	2.06%	100.00%		

Institutions which operate on an accrual basis will have set aside funds to provide for encumbrances, but it is inevitable that some will never come to charge and should be cancelled, while others may come in at a higher figure than was estimated. If there is also either a time limit or a money limit on their coming to charge, it may be well to review all very old outstanding orders and cancel those which seem unlikely to be received. Accrual accounting also requires the maintenance of parallel sets of accounts for the fiscal years concerned. This practice may cause problems when items from both years are billed in a single invoice or when credits are received against prepayments.

The final report is a stewardship accounting. It should show how close the collection development program came to meeting its goals. The report should be accompanied by explanations and comments whenever appropriate. A stewardship accounting is somewhat different from an annual departmental report in that it deals only with fiscal matters and concerns only the current year. Substantial variations from expected patterns may influence

TABLE 11.2   Library Materials Budget
Public Library
Year-End Expenditure
(Preliminary)

Area	Books	Standing Orders	Serials	Data-bases	Media	Total	Percentage of Total
REFERENCE	$ 13,110	$18,250	$ 5,270	$14,800	$ 500	$ 51,930	19.73%
ADULT							
Nonfiction	43,600	0	0	0	3,200	46,800	17.78%
Business	3,600	2,500	3,700	3,300	1,000	14,100	5.36%
Careers	2,000	500	2,200	1,900	700	7,300	2.77%
Periodicals	0	0	56,250	0	0	56,250	21.37%
Audiovisuals	0	0	0	0	10,000	10,000	3.80%
Gen. Fiction	31,500	0	0	0	0	31,500	11.97%
Mystery	2,000	0	0	0	0	2,000	0.76%
Romance	2,000	0	0	0	0	2,000	0.76%
Paperbacks	2,200	0	0	0	0	2,200	0.84%
Rental	[7,500]		0	0	0	[7,500]	
Large Print	3,590	0	0	0	0	3,590	1.36%
Subtotal	90,490	3,000	62,150	5,200	14,900	175,740	66.76%
YOUNG ADULT							
Nonfiction	3,300	0	650	0	0	3,950	1.50%
Fiction	6,100	0	0	0	0	6,100	2.32%
Audiovisuals	0	0	0	0	4,000	4,000	1.52%
Subtotal	9,400	0	650	0	4,000	14,050	5.34%
CHILDREN							
Reference	2,700	0	1,100	2,200	0	6,000	2.28%
Nonfiction	3,010	0	0	0	0	3,010	1.14%
Fiction	5,250	0	0	0	0	5,250	1.99%
Picture Books	6,315	0	0	0	0	6,315	2.40%
Audiovisuals	0	0	0	0	960	960	0.36%
Subtotal	17,275	0	1,100	2,200	960	21,535	8.18%
GRAND TOTAL	130,275	21,250	69,170	22,200	20,360	263,255	100.00%
PERCENTAGE OF TOTAL	49.49%	8.07%	26.27%	8.43%	7.73%	100.00%	
Over/under Expenditure	−325	250	2,070	500	−1,740	−755	

new allocations, and the amount of outstanding orders will affect the ways in which the current year's budget can be allocated.

Notes   1. Nancy Gibbs, "It's Hard Work Spending Money: Handling Budget Aberrations," in *Proceedings, Conference on Acquisitions, Budgets, and Collections,* compiled and edited by David C. Genaway (Canfield, Ohio: Genaway and Associates, 1991), 113–22.

2. In "Books in Limbo," a paper presented at the 1991 Charleston Conference, Arlene Moore Sievers addressed these and similar issues. If, as she suggested, more than 50 percent of dealer reports are in error, the librarian may indeed be able to bring in books that can be paid for in the current year rather than left for a later year.

Chapter 12

Review and Summary

Budgetary control is a continuous process requiring both broad concepts and attention to detail. The library materials budget provides a unique setting in which both play important roles. The budget itself gives reality to the ideals which guide the library in its service to users. For this reason it is essential not to be constrained by outmoded ideas when change is needed. At the same time, unnecessary change should be avoided since the library depends on the continuing flow of acquisition activities. In a way change and continuity are the yin and yang of budgeting and must always be kept in mind.

Budgetary Goals

The goal of any library materials budget is to ensure that the needed materials are available in a timely manner. Orders must be processed promptly, and dealers or publishers must respond in the same way. Achieving these goals depends on cultivating good relations with dealers and on good internal processes. Any acquisitions department should be organized to support both.

The first requirement is to set up a library materials budget that addresses the concerns of the library. The budget should show both subject and format provisions, since these will differ by subject. In addition, if the objectives of the library include both ownership and access, the library should have a budget which provides allocations for each kind of purchase. The balance will be determined by the level of need for information on the spot and the level to which students or faculty can use delayed information. Although the choice may be problematic, it can be assisted by historical records of reference and circulation transactions.

The second requirement is to set up a budget which takes into account changes in the information world. There may have been shifts of format or changes in the way in which information is packaged, or there may now be new alternatives available to the library. Unless these are taken into account when setting up the budget, it will not meet the library's requirements. The effects may extend beyond the library materials budget proper and impinge on reference and circulation services.

Changes in institutional objectives and programs may affect library objectives. If the school or community decides to stress other priorities, the library budget may be reduced. Similarly, if the members of the community move towards other interests, the library materials budget will need to be modified.

Only by working through these considerations can a library develop a responsive budget. Responsiveness is needed to justify continuation of adequate funding.

Monitoring

Once the budget has been set up, progress in spending it must be monitored. Here also there is a need for responsiveness to change—to meet real as against ideal needs—or to shifts within the publishing world. No budget is set in stone. It is at best a guide for the year it covers. If some deviation is in the best interests of the library and its parent institution, then changes should be made.

There are many players, not all of them within the library, and all need to be kept informed about the state of the budget. Selectors play a major role in building collections, but they cannot perform at their best if they are not told about changes in available funds. Budget officers, both inside and outside the library, need to be kept aware of library needs and problems. Library-materials buying is a continuous process and not amenable to sudden shifts in funding. The library must be user oriented and should always be able to point to what its users are achieving in order to justify its budgetary demands. There are inevitably shifts over time in what is being taught or researched; the public's interests change; and there are always new kinds of materials and new media. Publishers, dealers, and other members of the information industry also play an important part in determining what the library can or cannot do with its funds.

Effects of Price Increases

The main fact of library life has been the steady high rate of price increases for library materials, which has led many libraries to recast their collecting strategies in order to use steady-state budgets more effectively. During the early 1990s there appears to have been a substantial shift from buying "just in case" the item may be needed to "just in time" (buying only when an actual need has been expressed). This kind of change can be expected to continue, even to accelerate, as libraries come to rely more on the increasing numbers of ways to access rather than to buy materials.

Although the electronic dream may be slow in coming, many administrators are beginning to act as though it were already here. Libraries of all kinds have felt great pressure to experiment with electronic systems of information delivery. Contracts for service may become as common as direct purchases, but there is little evidence that library budgets are being conceived in ways necessary to support such a change.

Keeping Accounts

The mechanics of handling accounts are seldom stressed either by libraries or by library schools, but it is the budget that gives reality to any program or project. Careful attention to records and to record keeping is an essential part of collection management because only in this way can it be determined whether the library is truly meeting its goals. Good financial reporting cannot make up for lack of money but it can help prevent a disaster, as when funds run out before the end of the year. The repeated budget assessments that have become part of the education and local government scene can be handled properly only if the library has excellent knowledge of its financial status.

Accountability

Accountability has become a watchword. Without the presentation of reliable financial reports, a library cannot be accountable. Library materials represent the principal budget area where there is much flexibility to accommodate programmatic and financial changes. A good financial history is inestimably valuable in making decisions about the future. Only by knowing where you have been can you see where you may be going. Although electronic systems can reduce much of the burden of record keeping, and there is much good evaluative software available, decisions about the institution will continue to be made by people, and those people should be as knowledgeable about money as about books. Financial planning is continuous and cannot take place in a vacuum. Budget planners need to be informed about goals and needs, but those who set objectives also need to be realistic about money. The wise use of money should be an objective for any library. It represents the medium that can be transformed into collections for use, now and in the future. The library collection represents one of the most important of institutional investments and should be protected against unthinking devaluation, whether by those who have been called "technovandals" or those who see the saving of money as an end in itself.

Glossary of Accounting Terms and Phrases

This listing makes no claim to be comprehensive. For further information, readers should consult any recent accounting textbook. Readers are also referred to *Primer of Business Terms and Phrases Related to Libraries*, edited by Sherman Hayes (Chicago: Library Administration Division, 1978). The book was sponsored by the Budgeting, Accounting, and Cost Committee, Library Organization and Management Section, Library Administration Division (now Library Administration and Management Association).

Account. The record of expenditure in any specific category—e.g., books, serials—or a subdivision thereof—e.g., history. The term is often loosely used to refer to the actual category.

Account balance. The amount available for further expenditure—i.e., total less expenditure to date.

Accounting cycle. The complete sequence of procedures which record transactions during a fiscal period.

Accounting period. The period of time within which reports are prepared, most commonly a month.

Accounts payable. Payments due for services or materials received by the library. In this context, the term refers to invoices received for library materials but not yet processed for payment.

Accounts receivable. Not usually a matter of concern in library materials budgets, this term refers to payments due for services rendered or goods sold.

Accrual-basis accounting. The reporting of all income and expenditures that relate to a specific fiscal period, regardless of when they actually occur.

Adjusting entry.   An entry required in an accounting period to record an internal transaction and bring the record up to date. Such entries are often required to record transfers between accounts.

Allocation.   In library parlance, the division of the library materials budget among subjects, departments, or formats.

Appropriating authority.   In most cases this will mean the next highest level of government, but may sometimes refer to Federal Government action, for example most of the educational and library programs that provide funds for individual libraries.

Appropriation.   The library income that results from the action of the controlling authority, e.g., the town or city council or the institution of which the library is a part. The term is most commonly used in relation to the assignment of public funds by a government authority.

Approval plan.   Contract between the library and a vendor to supply materials within a set of prescribed limits. The items supplied are subject to return by the library as outside the prescribed scope, duplicates of materials already owned, or for other reasons. A plan may also carry special provisions concerning discounts, price limits, or other specifications.

Assessments.   Amounts by which budgets or specific accounts are reduced in the course of a fiscal year because of a revenue shortfall. They may be expressed in dollar or percentage form and may be general or confined to certain kinds of expenditures.

Audit.   The systematic evaluation of procedures, operations, and cash records to establish whether they conform to established financial criteria. In most cases auditors are external to the library.

Authority to purchase.   While it may seem clear that the library has the authority to make purchases, it may have authority in some situations— e.g., the purchase of library materials—but not in others—e.g., the purchase of capital equipment. Authorization may become quite complicated in the case of such purchases as CD-ROM work stations or the leasing of electronic databases. Library materials are usually seen as "outside the system"—i.e., they do not require individual purchase orders—but this is not always the case.

Balance of an account.   The difference between the debits (e.g., purchases) and credits (e.g., credit notes or refunds) that have been posted to a specific account. The balance may be thought of as unspent funds.

Bidding.   The process by which quotations are received from various vendors or dealers on one or more items to be purchased. Bidding is most often used in purchases of serials subscriptions, but some state agencies require that all materials be sent out to bid in the hope of gaining major concessions, e.g., higher discounts. Such a process may be informal or formal. The latter is recommended as assuring greater neutrality on the part of the library. It may not be necessary to rebid major contracts for the supply of materials every year, but it is desirable to review the terms of all major contracts periodically. *See also* **Approval plan.**

Book.   Strictly speaking, a book is a *codex,* i.e., a separately published, separately bound publication complete in itself. However, the term *book* is often loosely used to refer to nonserial paper publications including, for example, pamphlets. The term *book budget* is often used for the entire library materials budget. This usage is in fact erroneous, particularly now that many nonpaper formats are included.

Bookkeeping.   The process of recording debits and credits in accordance with established principles.

Budget.   The term most commonly used to refer to the funds available to the library for its activities within a prescribed period. A budget may be controlled in various ways, depending on the actions of the controlling authority. For example, salary savings may revert to the state, or there may be proscriptions against overexpenditure in specific categories without prior approval. In the broadest sense, a budget is a plan of operation for the period covered.

Budget categories.   Most commonly, allied kinds of expenditures—e.g., salaries, books, equipment. Budget categories may also be grouped as operating or capital expenditures, referring to everyday activities or to the purchase of assets that will last beyond the actual budget period involved. Despite the permanence of library materials, it is uncommon for them to be considered capital assets. There is no clear explanation for this custom, but it probably arose because the expenditures incurred for each item are relatively small. Few line-item or program budgets subdivide library materials by format, even though the library itself will have to do so in order to monitor expenditures.

Budget justification.   The process of developing reasons for a budget request, through reliance on statistics, goals, arguments, and the like. The result is a statement supporting the actual expenditure figures presented.

Budget performance record.   The comparison of actual expenditures with the budgeted amounts, which becomes the final report.

Calendar year.   The usual January 1 to December 31 year, which seldom coincides with a fiscal year. In some instances, such as special grants, calendar-year accounting may be used.

Capital budget.   The budget for fixed assets, such as buildings and equipment. This budget is usually associated with long-term planning but may include some amounts for small equipment, repairs, and the like, which may be subject to variant purchasing routines.

Cash basis accounting.   The accounting method that reports all revenue and expenditure figures during the period in which they occur. The resulting record does not include any encumbered purchases.

Chart of accounts.   A listing of all the accounts and subaccounts used by the parent institution. These are usually coded by the use of letters or numbers or a combination of the two. Very few such charts provide for the subdivision of the library materials budget by subject or department, but appropriate codes are usually available.

Contingency fund.   An amount set aside, usually at the highest budget level, to provide for unexpected or unplanned expenditures. Such a fund may be set up within the library materials budget to provide for the differing effects of inflation or for possible major purchases.

Cost accounting.   This procedure allocates all costs, direct and indirect, to some program or project. Cost accounting may be needed to support the allocation of indirect costs within the library. In the case of library materials, the procedure would take into consideration all processing costs and assign these to the costs of the materials purchased.

Credit memorandum.   The form used by a vendor to inform the library that a credit has been posted against the library's account—say, for materials returned or to adjust the price charged.

Discount.   The amount by which the recorded price of a purchased item has been reduced by the vendor or dealer. The general rate of discount is often the object of bargaining between libraries and major vendors. These rates are variable. Occasionally special discounts are allowed to retail booksellers, and these usually differ from those allowed for wholesalers or for direct purchase.

Encumbrance.   A commitment to incur expenditures at a future time, mostly used by nonprofit enterprises. An encumbrance is both a promise to pay and a commitment against available funds—the latter to prevent overpurchasing. When the item is received, the encumbrance is removed, and the payment becomes an expenditure.

Endowment funds.   Funds whose donors have stipulated that the donated capital will remain intact and only the earnings on the investment may be spent. These may be stand-alone funds or commingled by the parent institution to obtain a better rate of interest. The latter course is not available when the fund is composed of specific stocks or other investments which may not be changed.

Financial forecast.   A statement indicating plans and expectations for the future. In a sense the annual budget is such a document.

Financial report. The report which shows operating conditions, income statements, and expenditures, usually accompanied by remarks explaining achievements and deviations, if any, from the original budget.

Fiscal year. An accounting period of twelve consecutive months used as the operating basis for the institution. The most common such year is July 1 through June 30. The federal government, however, operates on a fiscal year from October 1 through September 30. A grant may be received to be spent over a period of years which do not correspond with either of the above, requiring that a separate accounting year be used for reports on that grant. It is necessary to be aware of what fiscal year is involved in any set of accounts and to keep the records for each fiscal year separate.

Funds. Used loosely to refer to all available money, the term actually applies to amounts set aside for specific purposes or activities.

Inflation. The rise in an economy's general level of prices. Inflation is a particularly important factor in purchases of library materials, which regularly increase in price at a rate greater than the economy as a whole. Tables show this increase as a percentage based on either the previous year or a chosen base year.

Internal check. The design of accounting transaction flow to protect against fraud. Internal checks ensure that no single person or group has exclusive control over any one transaction.

Invoice. The document supplied by the vendor stating the items covered, the prices, and the terms—e.g., service charges applied, or discounts given for payment before a given date. After being processed by the library, the invoice will be accompanied by a voucher, also numbered, which will state the account number and other data required by local accounting conventions.

Lease. An agreement to use materials for a specified period of time. Although once uncommon in library materials budgets, leases are now mandatory for many databases. The contents do not become the property of the library, which will pay an agreed-on annual sum for their use. For the most part, leases resemble serials subscriptions, but they may also carry use charges based on the number of uses or other contractual liabilities.

Management information system (MIS). A system, usually automated, that provides management with data for use in planning and controlling activities.

Object classification. A specific type of expenditure in the chart of accounts—e.g., 3310-500-127, where 3310 = Library, 500 = Library Materials, and 127 = Binding.

Operating budget.   The budget which covers recurrent activities, as opposed to capital or endowment funds.

Program budget.   A budget where categories of funding and expenditures are arranged by programs or services.

Purchase order.   The official document authorizing a vendor to provide goods or services, the purchase order is the basis of a contract between supplier and purchaser.

Requisition.   Where an institution has a formal procedure for the purchase of certain types of materials, such as furniture or supplies, this form requests that the agency concerned proceed to purchase the item requested. Library materials are usually exempted from this procedure.

Reserve fund.   Another name for a contingency fund. The reserve fund may be formalized or simply represent a certain amount of money held back for contingencies.

Standing order.   An arrangement whereby a publisher or dealer agrees to supply all titles published, for example, in a series or by a specific publisher.

Subscriptions.   Agreements to purchase all the issues of a periodical or serial without the need to supply orders for each issue. Subscriptions are usually annual but may be for longer periods.

Unit costs.   A standard value applied to all transactions within a given category. The most common example is mileage costs for travel, but libraries may develop standard costs for books purchased by category or subject.

Voucher.   The official form that authorizes payment of the amount specified from a specified account.

Zero-based budgeting.   A budgeting concept that requires all agencies to start from zero and estimate budget data as if there had been no previous activities on which to base estimates, and to justify all requests for funding.

Bibliography

Allen, Geoffrey G. "The Management Use of Library Statistics." *IFLA Journal* 11 (1985): 211.

Alsbury, Donna. "College Book Price Information." *Choice* 30,7 (1993): 1083–89.

Association for Library Collections and Technical Services. *Collection Management and Development Guidelines.*
    No. 1. *Guide to Writing a Bibliographer's Manual.* Chicago: ALA, 1987.
    No. 2. *Guide to the Evaluation of Library Collections.* Chicago: ALA, 1989.
    No. 3. *Guide to Written Collection Development Policy Statements.* Chicago: ALA, 1989.
    No. 4. *Guide to Budget Allocation for Information Resources.* Chicago: ALA, 1991.
    No. 5. *Guide to Review of Library Collections.* Chicago: ALA, 1991.

Atkinson, Ross W. "Old Forms: New Forms." *College & Research Libraries* 50 (1989): 507–20.

Baumol, William J., and Matityahu Marcus. *The Economics of Academic Libraries.* Washington, D.C.: American Council on Education, 1973.

Berry, John N., III. "Redwood City Public Library." *Library Journal* 117,11 (1992): 32–35.

"Book Price Indexes." *Library Resources & Technical Services* 20 (1978): 97–98.

Brazell, Troy V., Jr. "Comparative Analysis: A Minimum Music Materials Budget for the University Library." *College & Research Libraries* 32 (1972): 110–20.

Brinkman, Del. "Some Thoughts on Maintaining University Libraries at State-Supported Institutions." *Scholarly Publishing Today* 1,3/4 (1992): 6–7.

Brownson, Charles W. "Modeling Library Materials Expenditure: Initial Experiments at Arizona State University." *Library Resources & Technical Services* 35 (1991): 87–103.

Buckland, Michael K. "Library Materials: Paper, Microform, Databases." *College & Research Libraries* 49 (1988): 117–22.

Budd, John. "Not What It Used to Be: Scholarly Communication Then and Now." In *Scholarly Communication in an Electronic Environment,* edited by R. S. Martin. Chicago: ACRL, 1993, pp. 1–19.

Campbell, Jerry D. "Academic Library Budgets: Changing the Sixty-Forty Split." *Library Administration & Management* 3 (1989): 77–79.

Chamberlain, Carol E. "Fiscal Planning in Academic Libraries: The Role of Automated Acquisitions Systems." *Advances in Library Organization and Administration* 4 (1986): 141–52.

Chen, Ching-Chih. *Zero-Base Budgeting in Library Management: A Manual for Librarians.* Phoenix, Ariz.: Oryx, 1980.

Christensen, John O. "Cost of Chemistry Journals to One Academic Library, 1980–1990." *Serials Review* 15,8 (1992): 19–33.

Christianson, Ellory. "When Your Parent Dictates Your Accounting Life." *Bottom Line* 7,1 (Summer 1993): 17–21.

Clapp, Verner W., and Robert J. Jordan. "Quantitative Criteria for Adequacy of Academic Library Collections." *College & Research Libraries* 25 (1965): 371–80.

Dix, William S. "The Financing of College Libraries." *College & Research Libraries* 35 (1975): 252–57.

Dougherty, Richard M. "Are Libraries Hostage to Rising Serials Costs?" *Bottom Line* 2,4 (1988): 25–27.

———. "Exploding Myths: Clearing the Way toward a Redirected Campus Library." In *Proceedings, Conference on Acquisitions, Budgets and Collections,* edited by David C. Genaway. Canfield, Ohio: Genaway Associates, 1991, pp. 11–22.

Drucker, Peter. *Technology, Management and Society.* New York: Harper, 1967. *See* especially the chapter "Long-Range Planning," pp. 129–48.

Dunn, John C., Jr., and Murray S. Martin. "Cost Containment in Libraries." *Bottom Line* 5,3 (Fall 1991): 23–29.

———. "The Whole Cost of Libraries." *Library Trends* 14,3 (Winter 1994): 564–78.

Erickson, Rodney. "*Choice* for Collection Development." *Library Acquisitions: Practice and Theory* 16,1 (1992): 43–49.

Ferguson, Anthony J., Kathleen Kahoe, and Barbara List. *Columbia University Library Study.* New York: Columbia University Libraries, 1993.

Fong, Yen. "From Red to Black: Turning Around a Fee-Based Service." *Fiscal Facts* 2,2 (1990): 8.

Ford, Stephen. *The Acquisition of Library Materials.* Chicago: ALA, 1973.

Frazier, Stuart L. "Impact of Periodical Price Escalation on Small and Medium-Sized Academic Libraries: A Survey." *Journal of Academic Librarianship* 18,3 (1992): 159–62.

Gibbs, Nancy. "It's Hard Work Spending Money: Handling Budget Aberrations." In *Proceedings, Conference on Acquisitions, Budgets, and Collections,* edited by David C. Genaway. Canfield, Ohio: Genaway and Associates, 1991, pp. 113–22.

Goyal, S. K. "Allocation of Library Funds to Different Departments of a University—an Operations Research Approach." *College & Research Libraries* 34 (1973): 219–22.

Hayes, Sherman. "Budgeting for and Controlling the Cost of *Other* in Library Expenditure: The Distant Relative in the Budgeting Process." In *Financial Planning for Libraries,* edited by Murray S. Martin. New York: Haworth, 1983, pp. 121–31.

Higginbotham, Barbra B., and Sally Bowdoin. *Access versus Assets.* Chicago: ALA, 1993.

Higher Education Prices and Price Indexes, Update. Washington, D.C.: Research Associates of Washington, Sept. 1991–

Houbeck, Robert L., Jr. "If Present Trends Continue: Responses to Journal Price Increases." *Journal of Academic Librarianship* 13 (1987): 214–20.

Jaramillo, George R. "Computer Technology and Its Impact on Collection Development." *Collection Management* 10,1/2 (1986): 1–13.

Kirk, Thomas G. "Periodical Collections in College Libraries: Improving Relevancy, Access, Availability." *Journal of Academic Librarianship* 17,5 (1991): 298–301.

Kohut, J. "Allocating the Budget: An Economic Model." *College & Research Libraries* 35 (1974): 192–99.

Lenzini, Rebecca T. "Serials Prices: What's Happening and Why." *Collection Management* 12,1/2 (1990): 21–29.

Lester, Daniel W. "Twenty Years after Clapp-Jordan: A Review of Academic Library Funding Formulas." In *Financing Information Services: Problems, Changing Approaches, and New Opportunities for Academic and Research Libraries,* edited by Peter Spyers-Duran and Thomas W. Mann, Jr. Westport, Conn.: Greenwood, 1988, pp. 79–90.

Lynch, Clifford A. "Serials Management in the Age of Electronic Access." *Serials Review* 17,1 (1991): 7–12.

McCarthy, Paul. "Serial Killers: Academic Libraries Respond to Soaring Costs." *Library Journal* 119,11 (June 15, 1994): 41–44.

MacMillan, Gail. "The Balance Point: Electronic Journals: Considerations for the Present and the Future." *Serials Review* 17,4 (1991): 77–86.

McGrath, William E. "A Programmatic Book Allocation Formula for Academic and Public Libraries, with a Test for Its Effectiveness." *Library Resources & Technical Services* 13 (1975): 356–69.

McGrath, William E., Ralph C. Huntsinger, and Gary R. Barker. "An Allocation Formula Derived from a Factor Analysis of Academic Departments." *College & Research Libraries* 30 (1969): 51–62.

Magrill, Rose Mary, and John Corbin. *Acquisitions Management and Collection Development in Libraries.* 2nd ed. Chicago: ALA, 1989.

Martin, Murray S. *Academic Library Budgets.* Greenwich, Conn.: JAI Press, 1993.

———. "Budgetary Strategies: Coping with a Changing Fiscal Environment." *Journal of Academic Librarianship* 2 (1977): 297–302.

———. "Captain James Cook: Postage Stamps and Collection Management." *Collection Management* 18,1/2 (1993): 11–20.

———. "Cost Containment and Serial Cancellations." *Serials Review* 18,3 (1992): 64–65.

———. "The Implications for Acquisitions of Stagnant Budgets." *Acquisitions Librarian* 2 (1989): 105–17.

———. "The Invasion of the Library Materials Budget by Technology. Serials and Databases: Buying More with Less?" *Serials Review* 18,3 (1992): 7–17.

Martin, Rebecca R. "Special Collections: Strategies for Support in an Era of Limited Resources." *College & Research Libraries* 48,3 (1987): 241–46.

Massman, Virgil F., and Kelly Patterson. "A Minimum Budget for Current Acquisitions." *College & Research Libraries* 31 (1970): 83–88.

Medina, Sue O. "The Evolution of Cooperative Collection Development in Alabama Academic Libraries." *College & Research Libraries* 53,1 (1992): 7–19.

Metz, Paul. *The Landscape of Literature: Use of Subject Collections in a University Library.* Chicago: ALA, 1983.

————. "Thirteen Steps to Avoiding Bad Luck in a Serials Cancellation Project." *Journal of Academic Librarianship* 18,2 (1992): 76–82.

Metz, Paul, and Paul M. Gherman. "Serials Pricing and the Role of the Electronic Journal." *College & Research Libraries* 52,4 (1991): 315–27.

Naylor, Maiken. "Assessing Current Periodical Usage at a Science and Engineering Library: A dBaseIII+ Application." *Serials Review* 16,4 (1990): 7–19.

Nelson, Michael L. "High Database Prices and Their Impact on Information Access: Is There a Solution?" *Journal of Academic Librarianship* 13 (1987): 158–62.

Packer, Donna. "Acquisitions Allocation: Equity, Politics, and Formulas." *Journal of Academic Librarianship* 14 (1988): 276–86.

Palais, Elliot. "Use of Course Analysis in Computing a Collection Development Policy for a University Library." *Journal of Academic Librarianship* 13 (1987): 8–17.

Pearl, Nancy, and Craig Buthod. "Upgrading the 'McLibrary.'" *Library Journal* 117,17 (Oct. 15, 1992): 37–39.

Randall, William. "The College Library Book Budget." *Library Quarterly* 1 (1931): 421–25.

Richardson, Jeanne M. "Faculty Research Profile Created for Use in a University Library." *Journal of Academic Librarianship* 16 (1990): 154–57.

Sampson, G. S. "Allocating the Book Budget: Measuring Inflation." *College & Research Libraries* 36 (1979): 403–10.

Sartori, Eva Martin. "Regional Collection Development of Serials." *Collection Management* 11,1/2 (1989): 69–76.

Schad, Jasper C. "Allocating Book Funds: Control or Planning." *College & Research Libraries* 31 (1970): 155–59.

Scholarly Communication: The Report of the National Enquiry. Baltimore: Johns Hopkins University Press, 1979.

Sellen, Mary. "Book Budget Formula Allocation: A Review Essay." *Collection Management* 9,4 (1987): 13–24.

Snowball, George J., and Martin S. Cohen. "Control of Book Fund Expenditures under an Accrual Accounting System." *Collection Management* 3 (1979): 5–20.

Stanley, Nancy M. "Accrual Accounting and Library Materials Acquisition." *Bottom Line* 7,2 (Fall 1993): 15–17.

Talbot, Richard J. "Financing the Academic Library." In *Priorities for Academic Libraries,* edited by Thomas J. Galvin and Beverly J. Lynch. San Francisco: Jossey-Bass, 1982, pp. 35–44.

Tallman, Karen Dalziel, and J. Travis Leach. "Serials Review and the Three-Year Cancellation Project at the University of Arizona Library." *Serials Review* 15,3 (1989): 51–60.

Taylor, David C. "Serials Management: Issues and Recommendations." In *Issues in Library Management: A Reader for the Professional Librarian.* White Plains, N.Y.: Knowledge Industry Publications, 1984, pp. 82–96.

Traue, Jim. "Against the Grain." *New Zealand Libraries* 47,3 (Sept. 1992): 54–55.

Turock, Betty, and Andrea Podolsky. *Creating a Financial Plan: A How-to-Do-It Manual for Librarians.* New York: Neal-Schuman, 1992.

Wagner, Celia. "Book Prices, Publishing Output, and Budget Forecasting." *Against the Grain* 4,5 (1992): 5–6.

Warzala, Martin. "The Evolution of Approval Services." *Library Trends* 42,3 (1994): 514–23.

Werking, Richard. "Allocating the Academic Library's Book Budget: Historical Perspectives and Current Perspectives." *Journal of Academic Librarianship* 14 (1988): 140–44.

White, Herbert R. "Getting into This Mess Wasn't Easy! It Took a Lot of Effort on Our Part." *Technical Services Quarterly* 8: 3–16.

Wilson, Myoung Chang. "The Price of Serials Is Everybody's Business." *Bottom Line* 3,4 (1989): 12–14.

Winner, Langdon. *Autonomous Technology: Technics Out-of-Control as a Theme in Political Thought.* Cambridge: MIT Press, 1977.

Young, Harold Chester. *Planning, Programming, Budgeting Systems in Academic Libraries.* Detroit: Gale, 1974.

Index

Murray S. Martin is an accomplished author, educator, and consultant in collection development and other areas of library administration and finance. A chartered accountant as well as a librarian, he was University Librarian at Tufts University from 1981 to 1989, and was previously responsible for library collection development and financial administration at Pennsylvania State University. In 1989 he became adjunct professor at Simmons College (Boston) Graduate School of Library and Information Science.